Breaking Free

of Soul Cancers:
How to Find Them and Fight Them

By
Bill Fleming, Jr

Billy O. Fleming, Jr
Kindle Direct Publishing
©2023

For Molly

and Ethan

Table of Contents

Introduction 7

The "Deadly Sins" 9

Greed 33

Sexual Desire 43

Vainglory 51

Anger 61

Shame 69

Fear 79

Nostalgia (Grief) 87

Apathy (Acedia) 93

Pride 101

Epilogue—The Battle for the Soul 107

Prayer for Deliverance 111

Bad Thoughts Vs. Good Virtues 113

Introduction

When future generations look back on our time, they might see it as a dumpster fire.

First, the COVID pandemic spread around the globe, closing schools, churches, institutions, and all of society. With the pandemic came a variety of plagues--loneliness, depression, bitterness, heartbreaks, riots, and division, just to name a few. This was followed by global chaos and a sharp disagreement between people over what it meant to be free.

On one side were those who thought of freedom as safety from fear. They pushed for more masking, vaxxing, longer shutdowns, and social distance. They wanted protection from the government, and governments obliged with greater restrictions.

On the other side, some wanted social freedom. They wanted to make their own decisions and keep society open. To them, freedom meant an unrestricted life.

Like everyone else, I was caught up in this same argument. Then, something happened in our family that made my worries about COVID and the government seem puny by comparison.

One of my daughters got cancer.

"Cancer" is a terrible word, far more frightening than COVID. It rang like a death knell in our souls. Suddenly, COVID-19 meant nothing; being cancer-free meant everything. The only freedom I wanted was to hear that my daughter was cancer-free. Anyone who has faced cancer in themselves or their loved ones knows what I am talking about. We want the cancer to be gone.

Fortunately, my daughter's cancer is treatable. She is now getting treatment and making progress. But this brush with mortality made us think. Why is cancer so scary? Unlike bacteria or viruses, cancer is a homegrown horror. It begins with one of our own cells that misbehaves. It starts as an ordinary bone, skin, or other organ cell, but then something goes wrong. The cell disobeys. It goes wild, multiplying outside its usual place, growing, squeezing the life out of the tissue around it, upsetting the body's natural balance. The body does not immediately recognize its own cell as a threat. Antibodies that were created to destroy intruders accept cancer cells the same as healthy cells. It sucks up resources like a bratty child demanding food. It will keep growing until the body dies if it is not eliminated. We need medical intervention to destroy cancer once it begins.

This is not a medical book on cancer or medicine. It is about the spirit and the soul. I only bring up physical cancer to ask this question—are there such things as cancers of the soul? Are there parts of the soul, our immaterial self, that act like the cancers of the flesh?

I believe there are.

Our immaterial selves are made up of thoughts and feelings. God gave us many feelings and thoughts to fulfill the many purposes of life. He gave us love, hate, desire, aversion, happiness, and fear. Each feeling has a purpose in life; when they are balanced, they allow us to live happy, productive lives. But when a feeling gets too big, it outgrows its purpose and takes on a life of its own. Feelings like hunger, sexual desire, anger, fear, or despair can behave like cancers, pushing everything else out of the way. When this happens, we are unable to tame them. We need help. We must go to Doctor Jesus.

The "Deadly Sins"

The idea for this book began while I was having coffee with my pastor. Somehow, we started discussing the so-called "seven deadly sins" --*pride, lust, gluttony, greed, jealousy, wrath,* and *sloth.* My pastor casually mentioned that originally, there were eight of them.

"Eight?" I asked." Aren't there just seven? What did we leave out?"

No, he insisted. Originally, there were eight of them. The missing sin was *despair.*

This got me curious. I had always heard there were seven deadly sins, and I never heard despair called a sin. So where did that list of "seven deadlies" come from? Who made it? Moreover, were there any other "deadlies" we missed?

This started me on a journey of exploration. Ultimately, I read some of the church's greatest thinkers, who spanned almost all of its two thousand-year history.

Here is what I discovered. The seven deadly sins were not originally sins. They were not simple "do's" and "don'ts" but a psychologically complex system of good and bad thoughts. They were more like temptations than actual sins. If we gave into these temptations by sinning, they would dominate our lives, like cancer dominates the body.

The bad thoughts were connected to Satan and could be considered attacking demons in our souls. This list of bad thoughts was written not to make some legalistic list but to set us on the path of becoming psychologically and spiritually free. If we can deal with these bad thoughts as soon as we notice them, we can break their power and become free. But if we ignore them, they grow into soul cancers.

So, where did the list come from? Well, it started with a man named Evagrius.

Evagrius Ponticus was a Turkish monk who lived between 349 and 399 A.D. He became a priest at an early age and became famous—a rising star in the church. He was promoted to serve in the capital city of Constantinople under John Chrysostom—the most influential preacher of his age. Everyone celebrated Evagrius.

Even so, Evagrius climbed too far, too fast. When he got to Constantinople, he wasn't ready to deal with all the temptations of the royal court. He developed a serious crush on the wife of a nobleman, and word got out about his infatuation. Even though Evagrius did not fall into physical sin, it ruined his reputation. He was banished from the royal court.

To say he was sorry about this would be an understatement. His moral failure haunted him for the rest of his life. He entered a monastery to atone for his sin. Even in the monastery, he still felt guilty. He wanted to punish himself more, so he left the monastery to live as a hermit in the Egyptian desert. He thought isolating himself would help him get rid of his worldly thoughts.

Evagrius gave himself over to being holy. He spent at least four hours a day in prayer, got limited sleep, engaged in hard physical labor, owned nothing, and ate only one meal daily. Even so, his bad thoughts stayed with him. He still felt temptations of all kinds.

Evagrius' rigorous lifestyle is not an example we should follow. Still, his failure to achieve perfection teaches us a valuable lesson. We cannot escape our bad thoughts by withdrawing from the world. Bad thoughts come from the inside, not the outside.

Even if we run from the world and all its temptations, we still take our bad thoughts with us.

Eventually, Evagrius learned to live with his bad thoughts. He wrote a book he shared with his fellow monks to help them overcome their inner struggles. In his book, *On Thoughts,* he wrote that bad thoughts came from many sources--our sinful nature, thinking we learn from society, and direct attack by the Devil. The Spirit of God defends us from these thoughts. He does not take all our bad thoughts away, though. Instead, the Holy Spirit keeps them in check so we can recognize and stop them. But if we do not resist bad thoughts, they will destroy us. That is why soul cancer seems to be a more helpful way to describe these bad thoughts.

Consider Evagrius' problem—here is a monk sitting in his room in prayer and mystical meditation. Outwardly, he looks calm, even serene. But inside, a war rages: demonic spirits, lustful thoughts, despair, and anger attack his soul from within.

We are the same. The hardest battles we will ever fight are the ones within our souls.

In response to the temptations, Evagrius developed a model of resistance that still works today.

First, we must freely express our bad thoughts and give them to God. Evagrius listed eight of them, though there are more. We need to realize the thoughts that are plaguing our minds. But if we think we can defeat them, we are wrong. We must get into the habit of asking for God's forgiveness and help when we notice our bad thoughts.

There are two wrong ways of looking at our bad thoughts. The first is to pretend they do not exist. We do not like to admit that there is anything wrong with us. For example, we have all had the experience of being angry and denying our anger. Because we think of anger as bad, we can sometimes say, "I'm not angry," even when everyone around us knows we are. It is in our voice, our expression, and our body language.

The other wrong way to deal with a bad thought is to surrender. We know the bad thought is there and are prisoners to them. But instead of admitting failing and changing our ways, we give up, saying we will never change. We never change our thoughts because we do not believe our thoughts can be changed. We remain a prisoner to them forever.

Evagrius believed that bad thoughts could be overcome. To him, they were messengers of Satan--demons sent to torment the faithful. Like any demon, it can be rebuked in Jesus' name. If we resist temptations, they flee from us. The temptation may not entirely go away, but once we resist, the power of that temptation is broken in our lives.

Third, Evagrius encouraged us to summon the opposite virtues of these bad thoughts. We often make the mistake that good thoughts are just not bad ones. In reality, it is the opposite. Temperance is not the absence of gluttony; gluttony is the absence of temperance. To be generous is not the absence of greed; greediness is the absence of generosity. Think about the positive virtue and seek it; you will banish the bad thoughts from your mind.

Paul writes about this in Philippians 4:8: "Finally, brothers, whatever is true, whatever is noble, whatever is right, whatever is pure, whatever is lovely, whatever is admirable—if anything is excellent or praiseworthy, think about such things." These angelic thoughts are how we learn to control and eventually overcome the bad thoughts in our minds.

Changing our mood and behavior starts with changing our thoughts. Jesus showed the importance of our thoughts in Matthew 5: 25-28:

> "You have heard that it was said to the people long ago, 'You shall not murder, and anyone who murders will be subject to judgment.' But I tell you that anyone angry with a brother or sister will be subject to judgment. Again, anyone who says to a brother or sister, 'Raca,' is answerable to the court. And anyone who says, 'You fool!' will be in danger of the fire of hell.
>
> . . .
>
> "You have heard that it was said, 'You shall not commit adultery.' But I tell you that anyone who looks at a woman lustfully has already committed adultery with her in his heart.'

Murder comes from runaway anger. Adultery comes from runaway lust. Feelings lead to deeds. Therefore, we must learn to deal with private thoughts before they lead to public sins.

The List

Evagrius' list of bad thoughts went like this:
Gluttony, Greed, Lust, Vainglory, Anger, Nostalgia, Despair, and Pride.

This list was changed slightly by other writers, who added some more and combined others.

Eventually, Pope Gregory the Great made them into law with the seven deadly sins we now know and added a list of seven virtues to go with it. In making the list, Pope Gregory wanted to give a list of specific sins, which could have specific ways of penance with them. But this approach led him to see them more as actions than thoughts.

Evagrius' model of bad thoughts was later modified by others. Writing about eighty years later, John Cassian made another list of eight bad thoughts. Pope Gregory the Great, writing about a hundred years after Cassian, turned them into the "seven deadly sins" --*gluttony, lust, greed, pride, jealousy, sloth, and wrath*. These were set against the "seven noble virtues" --*chastity, temperance, charity, diligence, patience, kindness*, and *humility*. He changed them from "thoughts" to "sins" so priests, in hearing confession, could prescribe penance for them. But by turning them into outward sins, he focused on what we do, not what we think. This created more problems. Focusing on the results of bad thoughts instead of the thoughts themselves is like trying to hold back the flood without fixing the hole in the dam. Until we control our bad thoughts, they will always push us in the wrong direction.

It isn't sinful to have bad thoughts—only when we encourage them. It is normal, for example, to feel sexual attraction. Do not be surprised if Satan waves a sexy person before us like bait on a hook—don't bite! Being drawn towards a person sexually is not good or bad. It becomes bad when we think we cannot resist our bad thoughts.

Christians get in trouble when we think too highly of ourselves and believe we are beyond temptation. The world is full of forbidden pleasures, and our desire for them does not disappear until we leave this world. We must learn to live with temptation, continually wrestle with unruly desires, and find happiness and strength while struggling. Psalm 23 says, *"He sets a table before me in the presence of my enemy."* Soul cancers may always be with us, but we can be happy warriors, even in the fight.

Evagrius encourages us to look at the thoughts and feelings behind what we do. What were we thinking? What should we have been thinking? We cannot live a good, holy life without struggling against bad thoughts. Our minds and hearts will always be in battle.

We will look at Evagrius' eight bad thoughts, but we have added two more to his list—*fear* and *shame*. For each of the ten, we will ask three questions.

1)What was the original positive thought that grew into cancer?

2) What does it look like when it becomes a cancer?

3) What is the virtue that we can call upon to fight cancer? Or, to put it another way, what is the "angel" that fights the "demon" of the soul cancer?

1. Positive thoughts. There's nothing wrong with enjoying food. God made it enjoyable. There is nothing wrong with enjoying the world's material things, either. Anger is good, too, in its proper place, focused on injustice. Fear has its place, too. We do not want to remove feelings but enjoy them. They become soul cancers when they grow too big or strong, pushing every other feeling out of our heads.

When we treat lung cancer, we do not remove our whole lungs—just the parts of the lungs that are infected. We need our lungs! If we have brain cancer, we don't remove the brain. Likewise, when being ruled by anxiety, we should not pray that God will remove all fear, only the part that threatens to dominate our lives. Celebrate what is good about all emotions, even while we learn to ignore the free-floating and domineering parts of our feelings.

2. Cancerous thoughts. Soul cancers may become contagious, spreading to others. When a person is angry, it encourages angry feelings in others. We live in a world where soul cancers are called "normal." Things like promiscuous sex, anger, fear, and pride are celebrated in our world. It is no wonder that we have such a hard time escaping them. We need to follow God's standards instead of this fallen world if we are to master our own soul cancers. We cannot know when we are sick if we do not know what healthy is. A clear understanding of what "healthy" means enables us to tell when we are sick.

3. Angels versus demons. Identifying and seeking the corresponding virtue helps destroy soul cancers. We look at light and dark, for example, as opposites. But light isn't the absence of darkness—darkness is the absence of light. Just so, we often see the virtues as the absence of

Bad Thoughts Vs. Good Thoughts	
Gluttony	Temperance
Greed	Generosity
Lust	Chastity
Vainglory	Empathy
Anger	Forgiveness
Shame	Gratitude
Fear	Courage
Nostalgia	Joy
Despair	Hope
Pride	Humility

vices when it is the other way around. Chastity is not the absence of lust; lust is the absence of chastity. Temperance is not the absence of an addiction; an addiction is the absence of being temperate. The virtues we seek are positive, liberating experiences in themselves, which are denied us by our cancerous thoughts. Each positive "angel" frees us from the tyranny of a particular soul cancer. This becomes clearer as we discuss each one individually.

Finally, we must remember that we cannot free ourselves without help. When we are sick with a bad thought, we must go to Dr. Jesus. We must recognize the power of Christ, through God's Word and Spirit, to free us from our bad thoughts. God's power within is the only way we can overcome the oppression of soul cancers.

Ranking the Soul Cancers

We all have soul cancers, but they are not the same. We do not have the same ones all the time, either. A bad thought we struggle with may sometimes disappear or diminish, only to be replaced by another, working together like tag-team wrestlers in a wrestling match. The Enemy sends unique temptations to strike at our weakest points.

Think about these bad thoughts like pieces on a chess board. Satan moves one forward, then another, combining their powers together to block our spiritual progress. Just as chess has infinite combinations, so do spiritual struggles. No two people experience the same combination of spiritual temptations.

Evagrius saw bad thoughts like the rows of a chessboard. Up front are the pawns. They are the easier ones, but they are always the first ones we notice and are deadly in their own right. There are four of these--*gluttony, greed, sexual lust,* and *vainglory.*

Behind this first row is the second row. (I know the chess piece illustration doesn't work here, but bear with me. The second row is the "warning" row. Evagrius compares this row to a big dog chained to the front porch of a house. When we see the dog, we know that there's something inside that the owner is protecting. To Evagrius, the "big dog" was *anger.* When we get angry for no reason, we know that some other bad thought of anger is hidden within. To anger, I would also add *shame*. Shame is self-anger when our consciences feel bad, and we do not know why. We need to find the reason and deal with it. Shame becomes a soul cancer if there is no reason for shame.

The back row of soul cancers is the "power" pieces, like the knights, bishops, rooks, kings, and queens in chess. They are often hidden from sight at first. We see them and recognize their dangerous effect only when we begin to look deeply. These power pieces are *anxiety, grief, despair,* and *pride.* To win spiritual freedom, we must master this back rank. These pieces are the strongest and take a lifetime to master. Even so, God can deliver us, even from these powerful feelings.

The front rank—the "worldly" thoughts

The front-row temptations—gluttony, greed, sexual desire, and vainglory—are about our attachment to the things of this world.

Gluttony includes more than overeating and over-drinking; it includes all sensual pleasures and addictions. Gluttony is an obsession with the pleasures of the senses. Drugs, gambling, thrill—seeking, and video game addictions are a few manifestations of gluttony.

Greed includes more than just money and material goods. It is more about controlling the world and others through hoarding things, uncontrolled ambition, and dominating others.

Sexual lust is like gluttony or greed but with one different feature. Sexual desire always requires someone else, either real or imagined. Good sexual feelings lead us to long-term relationships. When sex is divorced from God's intended relationships, it becomes a destructive cancer.

Vainglory is a desire for approval from others. It encompasses prideful self-promotion and envy. Deriving our identity from God frees us from worrying about other people's thoughts.

The second rank—the "warning signs"

Anger, when appropriate, is good, but anger always brings problems. It may warn us of other things, but it can become problematic. When anger steps out of its boundaries, it becomes *wrath,* free-floating anger that is no longer about anything but a general state of mind. Wrath does not affect just us but everyone around us. We become paranoid, touchy, and abusive to others.

Shame is self-anger. Shame in its proper place leads us to repentance and change, but free-floating shame destroys our self-confidence and self-esteem. Before we can deal with our guilt through repentance, we must make it past shame and come to forgiveness and hope.

The third rank—the "rulers of the soul."

The back level of bad thoughts arise from deep misconceptions about God and the world. They are the source of all the other bad thoughts. There are four--*fear, despair, nostalgia,* and *pride.*

Fear by itself is not a problem. Healthy fear gives us the energy to run, fight, or endure. But when it becomes a cancer, we become frightened of everything. We become stuck in indecision, like a deer caught in the headlights. We either stay frozen or leap in aimless panic.

Despair is the absence of hope. It is when we cannot believe anything good is ahead of us, so we become numb to everything. We either become lazy and listless or restless and unstable. We search for something to hope for, but we find nothing. The future looks bleak to us.

Nostalgia is a word that has changed meaning over time. Nostalgia originally meant a sickness for the past or dominating grief. Nostalgia is not so much about loving the past but being unable to accept the present and future. Grieving is appropriate when we lose something or someone we love, but getting stuck in grief so we cannot get on with life is not.

Pride, or narcissism, is thinking only of ourselves. It is making ourselves the center of our own universe. A prideful person does not care about others but is blinded to everything but themselves and their problems.

Each of these bad thoughts has a corresponding angel. For gluttony, there is temperance; for greed, generosity; for lust, chastity; for vainglory, empathy; for anger, forgiveness; for shame, gratitude; for fear, courage; for grief, joy; for despair, hope; and for pride, humility. We can overcome our bad thoughts by developing our good angel virtues.

Let's see how by looking at these cancers one by one. We will start where Evagrius did, with gluttony.

Part 1 The Front Line: Addiction, Greed, Sexual Desire, Vainglory

Addictions (Gluttony)

"He said to the woman, "Did God actually say, 'You shall not eat of any tree in the garden'?" And the woman said to the serpent, "We may eat of the fruit of the trees in the garden, but God said, 'You shall not eat of the fruit of the tree that is in the midst of the garden, neither shall you touch it, lest you die.'" But the serpent said to the woman, "You will not surely die. For God knows that when you eat of it, your eyes will be opened, and you will be like God, knowing good and evil." So when the woman saw that the tree was good for food and that it was a delight to the eyes, and that the tree was to be desired to make one wise, she took of its fruit and ate, and she also gave some to her husband who was with her, and he ate." Genesis 3: 1-6

Gluttony is first on Evagrius' list because, to him, it is the place where all other sins start. Gluttony goes far beyond eating and drinking but is an uncontrollable desire to feel pleasure. These pleasures can come from food, drink, drug addiction, gambling, thrill-seeking, or video game addiction. *Any pleasure that becomes an addiction is a kind of gluttony.*[1]

The problem with addictions is not that we love some pleasure too much but that we are blind to all other pleasures of

---

[1] You notice, we do not include sexual pleasures here. Evagrius did see them as the same. We must acknowledge however that Evagrius and the desert monks do not seem to be as bothered by sexual desires as we are. Not that they were beyond these temptations--in the writings of the desert fathers we see many time that they could be deeply tempted by lust. However, they did not see them as any worse than other temptations. However, since sexuality is such a great temptation for us today, and since it has aspects of other temptations such as vainglory, we will discuss it later in a separate chapter.

life. While doing something that isn't good for us, we miss the other pleasures of the world. We eat so much that we cannot walk; we drink so much that our obsessions make us miss the pleasures of the world around us.

We stay addicted to one thing because we believe we have no other choice for fun. God fills the world with delights on every side. Only our lack of imagination and obsession with addictions makes it impossible for us to see how much pleasure is around us all the time. We could be taking long walks, getting a restful night's sleep, or doing something fun and creative. Controlling our eating and drinking allows us to enjoy the rest of life more fully.

We all have to eat. That is why gluttony for food is such a massive problem. We can't give up eating, but we can learn to do it in moderation.

Where gluttony begins

Gluttony begins as an ordinary, God-given, normal appetite. God gave us taste buds so we could enjoy our food. As long as we enjoy our food without overindulgence, we are fine. Ecclesiastes 3:12-13 tells us, *"I know that there is nothing better for people than to be happy and to do good while they live. Each of them may eat and drink and find satisfaction in all their toil—this is the gift of God."* God gave us five senses--sight, hearing, feeling, taste, and touch—to enjoy and experience the world. God associated all these sensual experiences with fun. We were not just created to live but to enjoy being alive.

Think of all the joys these five senses bring us—the taste of chocolate, laughter with friends, petting a puppy, the view of a mountain range in the distance, or the smell of roses. God did not have to give us any of these. He gave us pleasure everywhere we looked and in everything we tasted, smelled, saw, or heard.

What's wrong with that? Nothing, unless we try to repeat the same pleasure too often or take pleasures that are not ours. When we seek one pleasure too much, we forget all other pleasures. Some substances we eat and drink cause us to crave them more—sugar, alcohol, caffeine, and all illegal drugs—to name a few. The more we take them, the more we crave. Soon, no other taste or activity will satisfy. Then, we have an addiction, which can dominate and destroy our lives.

Not just food and drink but also sensual experiences can dominate our lives. Gambling and video games can stimulate our body's output of adrenalin—the "thrill" hormone- until we must always have that thrill.

Gluttony does not add pleasure to life; it takes pleasure away by drowning out our desires. We must remember the fun of exercise, company, or the joys of learning or accomplishing something new; all that remains is the pleasures of the belly.

Gluttony is about more than food and drink; it is about any pleasure we come to crave too much. Here are a few examples of other gluttonies beyond food.

The Many Faces of Gluttony

Gluttony of food

The early monks thought there was more to gluttony than how much we eat. John Cassian, for example, defined gluttony as:

- Eating outside of appointed times to eat.
- Eating until we are full.
- Being fussy about the kinds of food we eat.

In the *Screwtape Letters,* C. S. Lewis puts these words in the mouth of Screwtape, the demon, as he describes how to use his client's mother and her eating problems:

"Your patient's mother . . . is a good example. She would be astonished. . . to learn that her whole life is enslaved to this kind of sensuality, which is quite concealed from her by the fact that the quantities involved are small. But what do quantities matter, provided we can use a human belly and palate to produce querulousness, impatience, uncharitableness, and self-concern?. . She is a positive terror to hostesses and servants. . . . Because what she wants is smaller and less costly than what has been set before her, she never recognizes as gluttony her determination to get what she wants, however troublesome it may be to others. At the very moment of indulging her appetite, she believes she is practicing temperance. . .. The woman is in what may be called the 'All-I-want' state of mind. All she wants is a cup of tea properly made, an egg properly boiled, or a slice of bread properly toasted. But she never finds any servant or any friend who can do these simple things 'properly'—because her 'properly' conceals an insatiable demand for the exact, and almost impossible, palatal pleasures which she imagines she remembers from the past."[2]

How do we know when someone or something we love has become a "god" to us? When

- We cannot think of happiness in life without it.
- We neglect our duties for it.
- When we obsess about it when we do not have it.
- When it hurts our work, health, or family life.
- When we cannot quit or control our cravings, even though we know it is wrong.

[2] Lewis, C. S. *The Screwtape Letters* (pp. 87-92). HarperOne. Kindle Edition.

If we are addicted, we should get help. Just praying about it may not be enough. We may need medical and psychological help. We will need the help of a pastor, counselor, friend, or spiritual director. God clarifies in the Bible that we need other people to overcome addictions. *"Confess your faults to one another and pray for one another that you may be healed."* (James 5: 16). *"If we confess our sins, He is faithful and just to forgive us of our sins and cleanse us of all unrighteousness."* (1 John 1:9)

Online Gluttony

The gluttony of information affects us like the gluttony of food. We take in more than we can digest. When we digest it, we store it in brains that have become fat and sluggish on steady diets of junk facts, sold to us like junk food by greedy people who care nothing for us. We think of television, Facebook, Twitter, and TikTok as benevolent information and entertainment providers when all they do is sell our attention to the highest bidder.

Knowledge, like food, is only suitable for us if we can process it. If our minds cannot understand what we read by looking critically at it, then more information clogs our brains.

Knowledge is food for the brain, but how much do we need? Do we need to know what one celebrity is tweeting about another celebrity? Do we need every detail of some distant act of violence? Why should we know every detail of a political election where we have no vote?

Information overload troubles our souls but gives us no relief. It stirs us up but does not calm us down, like too much caffeine. Worse, it makes us believe that if we gain more knowledge, we can somehow fix the world around us.

To turn off the knowledge overload is not to become anti-intellectual. Developing the mind is a matter of skill rather than content. We are like children, feeding on sugary treats, thinking their sugar-addled tastebuds are enough of a guide for what's good for us. Not all education is good, and not all information is knowledge. Our connection to media and print is a choice. Accept the fact that all information takes time to ingest.

We will learn a valuable lesson from our ordinary activities as we fast or diet. We were not made to watch life but to live it. Information, stories, poems, books, and other materials are the raw thought resources that need to be thought through. Wait and work on the information before we pile on more.

The gluttony of thrill-seeking

Some people become so addicted to adrenalin that they can't stop taking chances. People with gambling addiction and kleptomaniacs find such satisfaction in risking their freedom or money that they cannot stop. They talk themselves into a false confidence that says they are too lucky or cunning to lose. But eventually, they do fail. Even so, they return to their destructive ways because the thrill itself is more important than winning or losing. They risk it all for thrills.

The problem with thrills is not that risk-taking is pleasurable but that it becomes their only delight. Thrill-seekers. Just as a glutton throws away his health for too much food and an alcoholic throws away his future for a drink, a thrill-seeker throws away their life by risking it for an extra shot of adrenalin. In doing so, they throw away all other joys in life--love, beauty, peace, happiness--everything good in life by throwing away life itself. All they enjoy is that jolt of adrenalin, and it is like heroin to them.

My own gluttony experience

Gluttony could have cost me my life. At one time, I weighed over three hundred pounds. I felt that weight in my body and mind. I was short of breath, tired, and on the verge of diabetes.

I am not fat-shaming, neither am I saying that all obesity is due to sin. This was my problem. I used food wrongly to escape from my troubles. It was my means of escaping the anxiety and troubles of the world by taking comfort foods. Instead of going to God, I went to the refrigerator.

I tried dozens of diets, but the problems started again when I stopped. I would lose forty or fifty pounds, and then my old eating patterns would reassert themselves. The appetite never went away.

I wish I could say my self-discipline was enough for me, but it wasn't. Eventually, I had my stomach shrunk surgically and lost over a hundred pounds. This surgery was a great help to me.

Before I had the surgery, I had to be willing. Jesus said, *"If your right hand offends you, cut it off."* It was not my hand but half of my stomach that had to go.

Ultimately, it was not the surgery or the lifestyle changes that the surgery forced upon me. I had to break the food addiction. At first, the change led to despair, as I realized I could no longer use food as a crutch. It felt like all joy had ended since food was my greatest joy. It was hard to imagine how I could enjoy life without all those bread and sweets.

I'm not alone in this. Addiction fools the mind into thinking there is no pleasure except the one we crave. This feeling of despair lasted for some time but eventually went away. Addiction also connects with our pride, fooling us into thinking we can beat it with more willpower. That is a lie. We always need help from the outside.

Once my addiction passed, my enjoyment of other things increased. I started enjoying exercise and walks in nature. I picked up some of my old hobbies as my energy increased. Much of the tiredness I attributed to age resulted from excess fat.

My taste in food changed. I became reprogrammed to healthier food. Carb addiction smothered my appetite for anything but junk food. It was good to discover other good things as well.

Looking back, I thank God for my food addiction. It has been my training ground for learning to trust God. Once we master our appetites for sensual pleasure, we become equipped for every other desire.

Temperance, the angel against addiction

With every bad thought, God gives a virtuous thought to counteract it. The positive virtue against gluttony is *temperance*. Rather than focusing on beating our addictions, let us use them to help us grow temperance.

Temperance is not a restriction but a celebration of personal freedom. Thomas Aquinas said we are not free to do evil--we are only free to do good. We do evil because we are slaves to our evil thoughts and desires. It requires no freedom to be a glutton, but we are only empowered by saying "no" to appetite.

But when we are temperate, we choose what we eat. Gluttony leads to many problems--diabetes, high blood pressure, joint problems, heart disease, etc. These problems stay with us long after the taste of that donut is gone. Why would anyone choose to be an addict? We do not choose this--we are dragged unwillingly down a punishing path. But temperance frees us. The longer we stay sober, the more we reap its benefits.

Temperance does not remove our addiction—it just dethrones it from our hearts. We are in charge with God's help. We become free to say "no" to appetite. Temperance is like a table set in front of our enemies. We know gluttony is there, but we can ignore it. We are strong enough to ignore it because we are enjoying temperance. We can look at it and walk away. When we exercise that option, we enjoy the fruits of temperance.

So, how do we attain temperance? Simple. The Holy Spirit gives it. It comes from the freedom we get from a relationship with Christ. We were created to have a relationship with God. When we do not, we are always hungry for something else.

My own experience continued

It has now been almost ten years since my surgery. My food addiction has not completely gone away. I have regained some of the weight I had lost. I still must occasionally diet to regain temperance. Even so, I've learned something important. Just because my body tells me it wants something does not mean I have to listen.

The world is full of so many joys that are not in the least addictive. I can enjoy a walk in the woods without huffing and puffing. I can mingle with others without being self-conscious. I can wear my old jeans. For these small things, I am grateful to God daily.

Paul says in Philippians 4:8 to think about good and beautiful things. The freedom of temperance is a very good thing. That Devil has not gone away, but I can ignore him. Food does not run my world anymore.

Greed

"Then God said, "Let us make humanity in our image, in our likeness, so that they may rule over the fish in the sea and the birds in the sky, over the livestock and all the wild animals, and over all the creatures that move along the ground. So God created humanity in his image; in the image of God, he created them; male and female, he created them. God blessed them and said to them, "Be fruitful and increase in number; fill the earth and subdue it. Rule over the fish in the sea and the birds in the sky and over every living creature that moves on the ground."

"Then God said, "I give you every seed-bearing plant on the face of the whole earth and every tree that has fruit with seed in it. They will be yours for food. And to all the beasts of the earth and all the birds in the sky and all the creatures that move along the ground—everything that has the breath of life in it—I give every green plant for food." Genesis 1:26-29

Greed is the desire to possess or control. This includes more than money and things but also other people and the world around us.

Greed starts as something good. Owning and controlling what is ours is not bad, but the gift God gave us at our creation. In Genesis 1: 28-30, we read:

"God blessed them and said to them, 'Be fruitful and increase in number; fill the earth and subdue it. Rule over the

*fish in the sea and the birds in the sky and over every living
creature that moves on the ground.'*

*"Then God said, "I give you every seed-bearing plant on
the face of the whole earth and every tree that has fruit with
seed in it. They will be yours for food. And to all the beasts of
the earth and all the birds in the sky and all the creatures that
move along the ground—everything that has the breath of
life in it—I give every green plant for food."*

God gave humankind the right to control the world with all
its plants and animals so we could improve it. We can change the
world from a disorganized jungle into an organized, beautiful
creation. A well-tended farm is even more beautiful than a
wooded hillside. When we see a farm, we know that some human
intelligence has tamed and improved the hillside, making it both
pretty and productive.

Genesis 2: 8 says, *"The LORD God had planted a garden in the east,
in Eden; and there he put the man he had formed."*

For there to be a garden, there must be a gardener. Adam and
Eve could not manage the whole earth, so God put boundaries to
their work. See Genesis 2:10-14:

*"A river watering the garden flowed from Eden; from
there, it was separated into four headwaters. The first name is
the Pishon; it winds through the entire land of Havilah, where
there is gold. (The gold of that land is good; aromatic
resin and onyx are also there.) The name of the second river is
the Gihon; it winds through the entire land of Cush. The
name of the third river is the Tigris; it runs along the east side
of Ashur. And the fourth river is the Euphrates.*

They were actually given the whole world. In time, I am sure they would have filled it. But for now, they only had to manage a specific tract of land. It was a large garden, but it must have still been manageable.

It is fun to imagine what would have happened if Adam and Eve had not sinned and bore children and grandchildren. Likely, God would have added more land to Eden as more people were born to tend to it. Eden was the training ground for future generations to spread across the land. Unfortunately, sin changed the plan.

We were created to create. Gardeners are artists, making beauty from the natural wild state of the world. The root desire God placed in us was to put our mark on the created world. We want to be busy making beautiful things. God was happy as long as Adam and Eve lived by the rules.

God put one tree within the Garden that was off-limits to them to test Adam and Eve. They could control or use everything else except that tree. Even so, they ate from the one tree they were not given. Adam and Eve did not learn to respect their boundaries but took what God told them to leave alone. As a result, God took away their tame garden and threw them into the wild with the other animals. They became tyrants instead of gardeners, taking more than they needed and controlling more than they were given. God had to change the natural world to defend it against the greed of humans. Genesis 3:17-19

> "Cursed is the ground because of you; through painful toil you will eat food from it.
> all the days of your life. It will produce thorns and thistles for you, and you will eat the plants of the field. By the sweat of your brow, you will eat your food."

This attitude of control and possession affected how they treated each other. God said to Eve. In verse 16, *"I will make your pains in childbearing very severe; with painful labor, you will give birth to children. Your desire will be for your husband, and he will rule over you."*

They will even be grasping and domineering towards each other. Instead of love and harmony, they will have greed and manipulation.

Greed is crossing God-given boundaries to use and control what is not ours. We may enjoy our wife, but not someone else's wife. We may raise our children, but not someone else's child. Boundaries between people must be honored.

This would not have happened had Adam and Eve respected God's boundaries. From the beginning, God gave them all they needed —whether they needed love, control, or security. All they had to do was ask.

The same is true of us today. We pray, "Give us this day our daily bread," and then we think that we, not God, give us everything. If we lack anything, we cannot conceive of God giving it or giving us the means to get it. We think the only way we can have anything is to take it from someone else.

"You have lost your mind!" people say if we believe God provides for us by His power alone. They accuse us of being lazy, foolish, and "so heavenly-minded that you're no worldly good." But Jesus says in Matthew 19:29, *"Everyone who has left houses or brothers or sisters or father or mother or wife or children or fields for my sake will receive a hundred times as much and will inherit eternal life."* God gives us all we need. There is no need for us to be greedy.

St. Francis of Assisi lived a life that was freed from greed. He gave away everything, even the clothes on his back, and lived as a beggar. He had no home or savings. Yet he was among the happiest men ever because he trusted Jesus always to provide. Once, some of his disciples found a bag of money lying on the ground and brought it to Francis. He ordered them to throw it in a dung pile! It was useless to them because God provided everything they needed. God is capable of delivering anything we need or want. *"For my God will supply all your needs according to His riches in Christ Jesus."* Phil 4:19.

"But isn't that foolish? Aren't you saying that we do not need to work?" We *don't need* to work; we *get* to work. We were created to make and create, and we are unhappy without something to do. For that reason, God gave us the job of providing for ourselves and our families. Ecclesiastes 2:24 says, *"A person can do nothing better than to eat and drink and find satisfaction in their toil. This, too, I see, is from the hand of God."* We cannot be happy without working.

He also gave us the task of helping others. We get great satisfaction from sharing with others. But when we forget that everything we have or will have is a gift of God, the soul cancer of greed and control remains with us. Greed starts when we stop trusting God.

Greed as Power

Greed shows itself in two ways—power and possessions.

Controlling others is a big temptation to Christians because we think we know better than them. We even believe we are responsible for others instead of God. That leads us to believe we can know what God wants another person to do. Instead of listening to God, we demand that they listen to us as we speak in God's name. But God does not give us the right to meddle in other people's affairs, nor does He give us the wisdom to know what He is doing in their lives.

We become meddlers in other people's business. We meddle because it makes us feel strong and smart because we are convinced our children don't know what's best for them, or because someone we know is always making the wrong decisions. We may meddle because we are afraid the world is spinning into chaos, and we think we can fix it. Whatever our excuses, we fail to respect other people's boundaries. Other people have the same right to act freely within our boundaries. People must answer to God, not to us. We must let people make their own mistakes and live with the consequences. Anything outside our boundaries is under God's control.

He has not told us to control our neighbors but to love them. We may cooperate with our neighbors through commerce and sharing. We may be put into a position of being a leader in a family or business. But even our leaders have no business expanding beyond the limits of their leadership. Boundaries must be kept in every area of life.

"Judge not, so that you will not be judged." Matthew 7:1. We have no business judging others.

If it is tempting to seek control over others, it is especially tempting to want to control our loved ones. We want to "fix" our children and our spouses. But if we try to fix someone else, we make ourselves their savior instead of Jesus. We become 'antichrists," people who take the place of Christ; our behavior becomes the opposite of God's, who allows us to make choices-- even bad ones—so we can learn how to make good choices.

Paul wrote in 1 Thess. 4:9-11: We encourage you, brothers. . . to seek to lead a quiet life, to mind your own business, and to work with your own hands, as we commanded you." "Mind your own business" comes from the Bible. It is listed in this verse as an example of how we love our neighbor. Love keeps within its boundaries.

Greed as possessing

Because we believe God won't provide, we must provide for ourselves, grabbing and holding onto as much money as possible. This makes us "hoarders" afraid to let go of anything because we think we will need it tomorrow. We do not give to others because we are convinced nothing will be left for ourselves.

The desire to own is one of the biggest problems in our culture. Here are some statistics that illustrate what I mean:

- The average American home contains more than 300,000 individual items. (LA Times)
- The average size of the American home has tripled in the past fifty years, twice that of most European homes. (NPR).
- Ten percent of American families require offsite storage to keep all their possessions.
- Americans have 3.1% of the earth's children but own 40% of the toys. (UCLA).
- The average American woman owns 30 outfits—one for every day of the month. (Forbes).[3]

Why do we need so much junk? Because we cannot trust God. We do not need that third lawnmower now, but we might need it one day—do we think lawnmowers will someday become scarce? Surely, we can trust God to repair or replace a lawn mower if the other two break down.

The more we have, the more we must protect. Guarding our possessions makes us prisoners of them and keeps us from being free. It is hard to trim down our possessions, but if we do not, they'll smother us.

Seven <https://www.becomingminimalist.com/clutter-stats/>

Remember Jesus' words: *"Do not lay up your treasures on earth, where moth can eat, rust can corrupt, or thieves can breathe in and steal. But lay up your treasures in heaven."* We do not have to guard what we do not have. Ridding ourselves of stuff enables us to enjoy freedom now.

Generosity—The angel against greed

Once, I was with a mission group in Africa, in a very poor city. After the service, the pastor invited us for dinner at his home. He also invited several of his of his elders.

The pastor's home was very poor, and he did not have much food. I considered opting out because I did not want to burden the host. However, a seasoned missionary explained to me that this would be an insult to the pastor. In their culture, the ability to be generous was one of the greatest joys of life.

Generosity is not just a lack of greed but a great experience. People love to give when they have the means to do so. Generosity is the freedom to give without thinking about it. Generosity is an attitude of life that flows from the understanding that we already have enough. We can fulfill Jesus' words, *"Give, and it will be given to you. A good measure, pressed down, shaken together, and running over, will be poured into your lap. For with the measure you use, it will be measured to you."*

In Matthew 25:14-26, Jesus tells the parable of a rich man who gave bags of gold to three servants. Two invested in them and were rewarded. The third buried his gold in the ground, getting no interest or reward. He was afraid of losing the money, so he hid it. So much of our greed is really about fear. By faith, people who trust God know that God will provide so they can afford generosity.

God does not promise to make us rich if we are generous because it would make God a friend of greed. God has already blessed us with His protection. We do not have to seek His blessings because we already have them. All we have to do is see how blessed we already are. Being generous to others helps us to recognize this and enjoy life more.

Is it better to have lots of money, or not to need any money? A generous Christian will not give till it hurts because it never hurts him to give.

Generosity is a selfless attitude, living without worry for ourselves. Instead, we can spend all our time giving to others. Listen to St. Ignatius Loyola's prayer of generosity:

> *"Eternal God. . .Teach me true generosity.*
> *To serve You as you deserve,*
> *To give without counting the cost,*
> *To fight heedless of wounds,*
> *To labor without seeking rest,*
> *To sacrifice myself without thought of reward,*
> *Except the knowledge that I have done Your will.*
> *Amen."*

We do not *have* to be generous; we *get* to be generous because God is continually generous. Generosity is a delightful pleasure any of us can have. Generosity is enjoying the freedom of God's eternal provision. The joy of generosity makes the pleasures of riches unnecessary.

Sexual Desire

"Do not be deceived: Neither the sexually immoral nor idolaters nor adulterers nor men who have sex with men nor thieves nor the greedy nor drunkards nor slanderers nor swindlers will inherit the kingdom of God. And that is what some of you were. But you were washed, you were sanctified, you were justified in the name of the Lord Jesus Christ and by the Spirit of our God." 1 Corinthians 6:9-12

Sexual desires were not included in Evagrius' original list of "bad thoughts." He included it under gluttony since it is a cancer of sensual experience. We will treat it as its own soul cancer for a couple of reasons: first, because of the havoc it wreaks on families and the world, and second, because it has one characteristic that separates it from other sensual pleasures. It is impossible to engage in sexual pleasure without connecting it, either in the real world or in our imagination, with other people. For these two reasons, it deserves treatment all on its own.

Good Sex

Sexual desire is a good thing. Without it, families would not exist. God placed sexual desire in us so there would be children, mothers, fathers, grandparents, grandchildren, aunts, uncles, and cousins. Unless human cloning becomes a thing, sexual desire will always be necessary to create the race.

The need for families is more important than our need for sex. Families are not just for reproduction. They are where we experience love, raise children, become educated, and care for the sick and the elderly. We all need a place where we are loved and welcome. Sex is only a catalyst that sparks the reaction that leads to a loving family.

Think of emotions like organs in the body. Sexual desire is part of the love system of our soul, but it is not an essential part. Some organs we cannot live without, like the heart or lungs; others we can live without. Sex is not necessary to us as individuals, but love is. Sexual love contributes to the development of family love, but it is unnecessary. Families are more important than sex. Where there is no sex, we still need a family.

God gave us sexual desire so it would lead us to something better. Look at Genesis 2: 18-24:

> *The Lord God said, "It is not good for the man to be alone. I will make a helper suitable for him." . . . But for Adam, no suitable helper was found. So the Lord God caused the man to fall into a deep sleep, and while he was sleeping, he took one of the man's ribs and then closed up the place with flesh. Then the Lord God made a woman from the rib he had taken out of the man, and he brought her to the man.*
>
> *The man said, "This is now bone of my bones and flesh of my flesh; she shall be called 'woman,' for she was taken out of man." That is why a man leaves his father and mother and is united to his wife, and they become one flesh.*

God did not create sex just for two people to come together, but so all people, whether sexually active or not, can find a home and family. Sex between two people starts a family, but love between relations builds something much stronger. Sexual love leads to love for children, fathers, mothers, and grandchildren. It is a shame that sex in our society is seen as a form of recreation to be entered into casually and only affects two people. The results of sexual union, when properly expressed within a heterosexual marital union, lead to a circle of love. Without that union, it leads to division and chaos.

Just as the Trinity is three persons in one Godhead, men and women are two sexes in one species. When the two sexes come together, they become "one flesh." The connection is so strong that they become almost one being.

Sex is not necessary for survival. A person can live a happy life without ever having sex with other people. Some expressions of sex may be pleasurable but forbidden. Almost everyone who has sexual desire will find it forbidden at times. Unlike other bodily desires, God created us so that our sexual feelings would be delayed until adolescence, when we come out of our childhood. He also caused sexual desire to diminish in old age so we could enjoy other things. Children and older people enjoy other things than sex—the love of family and friendship and a sense of innocence, to name a few. Sexual desire appears after puberty to encourage us to create new families and partnerships so we will enjoy creating our own families.

The Bible is clear on one point. Sexual desire is for heterosexual attraction in marriage, and it is not to be indulged for other purposes until a couple is cemented in marriage permanently and irrevocably. Until then, we learn to restrain ourselves. This restraint does not hurt us; it is not impossible but merely difficult. But then, what isn't?

In the Bible, sexual relations are confined to the marriage of men to women. Homosexuality and extramarital sex are mentioned in the Bible, but never in a good way. The Bible acknowledges that the sex drive is with us, but it forbids fulfilling that drive outside marriage.

Our sex drive is rooted in biology. The drive itself is the same for almost everyone. Even so, we must all learn to control that desire and express it as God intended, even if that means never fulfilling it at all.

This is the conundrum of sex for the Christian. God gave the ache, but He forbade its fulfillment except in heterosexual marriage. That means all of us, whether we marry or not, must learn to abstain at times. Why did He play such a trick on us to give us a desire and forbid its fulfillment?

One possible reason for this is that sex is never just sex. The Greek term for that desire—*eros*-- has a much larger meaning than the sexual act. It is one expression of our life force or energy that connects us to the world around us. The hormones associated with sexuality—testosterone and estrogen—are also released when we play sports, fight, nurture children, or hold puppies. Eros plays a part in every facet of life—building, creating, expressing ourselves, and sharing who we are and know.[4] By focusing eros only on sex, we are missing out on many other joys of life.

We do not need to have sex to be a fulfilled person. Not everyone is made for marriage. Many people live happy lives without it. Jesus lived this way, unmarried and happy. He calls such people "eunuchs." *"For there are eunuchs who were born that way, and there are eunuchs whom others have made eunuchs—and there are those who choose to live like eunuchs for the sake of the kingdom of heaven."* (Matthew 19:12) A person living celibate for the kingdom should be respected for their obedience to God and given an honored place in God's family.

One person who fits this category was the minister, theologian, and composer Isaac Watts. Watts never married. One

---

[4] For a longer and better discussion, see Tom and Bev Rodgers *Soul-Healing Love,*

woman fell in love with his mind through correspondence, but when she met him, she is reported to have said that although she admired the mind, she could not abide the box that contained it. Even so, Watts lived with the family of the Lord Mayor of London and became a beloved member of the family. Our families are flexible and should contain many who are not directly related to us.

When sex becomes a soul cancer

Our culture opposes the Christian view of sex and even promotes lies against it.

The first myth our culture pushes is that *not having sex is unhealthy*. This is not true. Hundreds of millions of people never have sex out of choice. Monks, nuns, and priests remain celibate their whole lives. Even so, studies have shown that they are among the happiest people on earth.[5] Until recently, most Christian couples married when they were both virgins. Until recently, no one would even suggest that it was unhealthy to be a virgin.

The second myth is that *celibacy is impossible.* Sexual restraint *is* possible because most of us already practice it. Husbands and wives may be married, but they resist adultery. Some of us still have saved ourselves for marriage. Widows and singles practice restraint all the time. The proof of celibacy is all around us.

A third myth of our culture is that *we can have sex without meaningful relationships*. Some couples try to convince themselves that they can have "open relationships" --lovers outside of marriage who satisfy their sexual needs with no strings attached. Experience usually proves this is a terrible idea. Apart from the dangers of sexually transmitted diseases and unwanted

---

[5] www.livescience.com/9542-monks-darn-happy.html

pregnancies, it is soon obvious over time that sex cannot be separated from intimacy. Sex makes two people one. Sex with multiple partners destroys a part of our soul and causes endless problems.

When sex, love, and intimacy are disconnected, it dehumanizes people. Pornography teaches young people to regard sex partners as disposable objects. Prostitution, pornography, human trafficking, and rape are problems created when we unhook sex and relationships.

A fourth myth is that *sex determines our identity.* In the early stages of sexual development, many people develop confused attractions. Some are attracted sexually to their sex. It is not unusual for adolescents to be confused about sexual identities.

Our culture insists on dividing people into groups based on sexual attraction. If they feel attraction to their own sex, they are called "gay," "queer," "lesbian," or "bisexual." Once they accept those terms, they become separated from those who do not feel the same attraction. This feeling becomes their identity. Our sexual desires are assumed to define who we are. Our "team" tells us that they must live a lifestyle that goes along with our temptations. Suppose a person chooses to get married despite their attraction or remain celibate. They are seen as being inauthentic, denying their "true selves."

But our temptations do not have to define us. A Christian lives according to God's commands. They have no other identity but as a child of God.

Sexual urges are always resistible. We choose to live a life different from our sexual desires, whether labeled "gay" or "straight." A child of God will always seek to keep sex within the limits of what God intends, even if it means remaining celibate forever.

But what about people who fail to practice sexual restraint? They are no different from those of us who lose our tempers, overeat, get greedy, or run away from our problems out of fear. We are weak people who all need forgiveness. People who lose their virginity can regain spiritual virginity by practicing chastity. In God's eyes, no difference exists between a former sinner and one who has never sinned. Mary Magdalene, likely a prostitute, was a virgin in God's eyes. There is no shame when we admit our sins, repent, and are restored.

We should do more than resist sexual temptation to be pure. We must actively practice its opposite—*chastity.*

Chastity

Chastity seems out of place in our modern world, so it's hard to realize how important chastity is in other societies. chastity is more than not having sex; it is a celebration of holy innocence, the feeling of being pure and clean.

Do you know that feeling you have when you get out of the shower—that tingly feeling of being fresh and clean? Do you know that sensation of waking up refreshed from a good night's sleep? Can you remember the glory of childish innocence, with a whole life of optimism and goodness before you? Then you know how chastity feels.

Chastity is restored innocence and purity, coming clean before God with nothing to hide and everything to discover. Chastity is freedom from the bondage of lust, liberty from past mistakes, and hope for a better tomorrow.

Is it hard to remain chaste? Of course! But it is much easier than the endless complications of *not* being chaste and better than living in the bondage of lust.

Anyone can have chastity, no matter what their past is. Christ forgives and cleanses our past sins. *"If anyone is in Christ, they are new creatures."* 2 Corinthians 5:17. When we repent and turn to God, we become chaste again.

Confession and cleansing should be part of our daily rituals, like bathing. Turn our temptations over to God. In time, He will strengthen our courage and resolve, and we will find it easier to practice chastity. We do not have to be run by our sexual temptations, whether heterosexual, homosexual, or bisexual. God can set us free, and we can rejoice in that freedom. Paul tells us this in 1 Corinthians 6:9-11:

> *Do not be deceived: neither the sexually immoral, nor idolaters, nor adulterers, nor men who practice homosexuality, nor thieves, nor the greedy, nor drunkards, nor revilers, nor swindlers will inherit the kingdom of God. And such were some of you. But you were washed, sanctified, and justified in the name of the Lord Jesus Christ and by the Spirit of our God.*

"And such were some of you." Paul may have written, "And such were all of you." If we are honest, we have all struggled with sexual desire and lost at some point. Even so, Christ can set us free, no matter how far we have gone.

Vainglory

*Fear of man will be a snare, but whoever trusts in
the LORD is kept safe.*
Proverbs 29:25

Finally, in the front rank of bad thoughts is *vainglory*.
Vainglory includes vanity and envy since it is all about how others
look at us. Vainglory is an excessive concern over what others
think. It is when our feelings of self-worth depend on being liked
by others instead of on our relationship with God.

The good side of vainglory

We all care about other people's opinions when we are
young. Our relationship with our parents, grandparents, and
siblings helps us. When we are young, encouragement and
correction from our parents help us develop as humans. When a
parent shows a child free and unqualified affection, that child
learns to expect the same unqualified affection from God. The
child gains the confidence to venture into the world and have
adventures. When a parent corrects a child, our devotion to them
teaches us to obey. Children see their parent's praise as a sign of
God's affection.

God also sends people who love, mentor, and encourage us
through our lives. Since we can't experience God's physical
presence, He sends people who represent Him into our lives. We
need connections to others our whole lives.

Other people serve as both mirrors and windows to us. As
mirrors, other people show us ourselves. Our close friends and
family know us better than anyone else, giving us a clear and

(mostly) positive view of ourselves. As windows, other people introduce us to the wider world, letting in different opinions, ideas, and other ways of feeling. They also keep us honest. They see us and hold us accountable to moral people if we go astray.

John Cassian wrote that vainglory might sometimes save us from a greater sin. If worrying about our reputations keeps us from committing vices such as fornication, gluttony, or greed, it may be a little help. It is not good, but it is the lesser of two evils. It is better to avoid sin, for God's sake, not because you are worried about your reputation.

If we worry about our reputation too much, we fall into vainglory. Other people make wonderful companions but terrible gods. When we obsess about pleasing others, we have put them in the place of little gods, setting them above the real God in our lives.

Those who guide, love, and protect us may be god-sends, but they are not God. God is the source of all we need, not people. He may send us comforters, but He is the best comforter. He is also our healer, deliverer, and friend.

The bad side of vainglory

Vainglory takes many forms.

One is *victimization*. We believe that other people have not treated us as we deserve. The biggest problem with seeing ourselves as victims is that we must also see ourselves as having no power. To be a victim is to be powerless and helpless before the opinions of others. We must always be looking for a "savior" to rescue us. But we are no longer victims when we take responsibility for our self-worth.

Another is *jealousy*, comparing ourselves to others, which may cause us to feel inferior and cheated. We may all occupy the same planet but do not live in the same world. What one person has or does not have has no bearing on who we are. We must learn to live in our heads, according to our standards, before we can willingly give ourselves to the standards of others.

Another voice is *attention-seeking*. Having lost our sense of personal God-worth, we seek worth in praise of others. We look for positions and honors to prove ourselves. If we do not get enough, we become bitter. We spend our time endlessly seeking human validation.

Vainglory is so subtle! It is the pet sin of preachers, teachers, counselors, and Christian leaders. It lurks in the background, waiting to pounce upon us, even amidst our best behavior. It sneaks up on us, even in the best of times, and ensnares us with a wicked collection of traps. Here are some ways vainglory traps us.

The "cool kids" trap

Every school had its "cool kids"— that clique of friends everyone wanted to join. Larger schools may have many cliques, each with a separate group of "cool kids"-- jocks, popular students, goths, rebels, smart kids, or computer nerds. Each has its own dress, slang, and behavior standards that make them feel like the "cool kids."

It doesn't stop with school. It's the same in businesses, churches, politics, and higher education. The more we look at the adult world, the more we realize that the "cool kids" never disappear. Anyone who has ever wanted to belong to a group knows the influence of the "cool kids" on our lives.

Running with the "cool kids" may get us ahead in the world, but God does not usually run with the "cool kids." Christians do not seek to be successful in this world but to rise above it. We do not need the best clothes, the biggest houses, or the highest position to be happy. Christians only need Jesus. If we are worried about measuring up to others, we have already swallowed the hook.

Christ came to save us *from* the world, not give us the world. He did not call us to rule this world but to make a new one with Him. In Christ's kingdom, He is King. He rules over us and does not need other leaders to accomplish this.

In John 16: 18-19, Jesus said: *"If the world hates you, remember that it hated me first. If you belonged to the world, it would love you as its own. As it is, you do not belong to the world, but I have chosen you out of the world. That is why the world hates you."*

And again in John 16: 1-3: *"All this I have told you so that you will not fall away. They will put you out of the synagogue; in fact, the time is coming when anyone who kills you will think they are offering a service to God. They will do such things because they have not known the Father or me."*

To follow Jesus is to be unpopular. We live by different standards than others, so we should not look to them for approval. Instead of asking God *why the world hates us,* we should ask why the world does not *hate us more.* If we are doing nothing that sparks disapproval from the world, we must be doing something wrong.

Christians sometimes excuse their desire to be one of the "cool kids" as a kind of witness. Jocks and class leaders influence more than loners and nerds, so we think if we are one of the popular ones, we can better share the Gospel or influence the world in a good way. Maybe we would, but it is more likely that *we* will be more influenced than be an influencer. Those who have the most impact on society dared to be different. Jesus stood outside the power structure of His day. He ate with sinners, but he did not become a sinner. St. Francis overturned the culture of his time while walking barefoot in a borrowed robe. "Fitting in" is probably the worst way to make a lasting difference.

The "pretender" trap

A second trap is *hypocrisy*. In ancient times, actors were not celebrities but slaves. They wore elaborate costumes that hid their entire body, like a mascot suit at a ball game. Their mask, helmets, and wigs covered them entirely. Plays were usually performed outside, so the actors must have been hot and uncomfortable sometimes. Still, their masters insisted they pantomime their parts before the crowd.

That is what Jesus meant when he used the term "hypocrite"—false-faces one. A hypocrite was a prisoner in a suit, unable to show his real face. As Jesus said in Matthew 5:

"Beware of practicing your righteousness before other people to be seen by them, for then you will have no reward from your Father who is in heaven. Thus, when you give to the needy, sound no trumpet before you, as the hypocrites do in the synagogues and the streets, that others may praise them. Truly, I say to you, they have received their reward. But when you give to people in need, do not let your left hand know what your right hand is doing so that your giving may be secret. Your Father who sees in secret will reward you.

And when you pray, you must not be like the hypocrites. They love to stand and pray in the synagogues and street corners so that others may see them. Truly, I say to you, they have received their reward. But when you pray, go into your room, shut the door, and pray to your Father in secret. And your Father who sees in secret will reward you. . .

"And when you fast, do not look gloomy like the hypocrites, for they disfigure their faces so that others may see

their fasting. Truly, I say to you, they have received their reward. But when you fast, anoint your head and wash your face, that your fasting may not be seen by others but by your Father who is in secret. And your Father who sees in secret will reward you."

This is what vainglory does to us. It makes us a prisoner in a false suit. We are afraid to show our real faces, so we are trapped into wearing another.

This happens when we cannot share our feelings or opinions or treat people as we want. We are trapped with a false face. The only way to escape our false costumes is to stop caring about the crowd. When we are afraid to be different, we become false.

The "mirror" trap

When I was a pastor, I visited many people's homes. I would try to give them all my attention when talking to them. But sometimes, I would get distracted. One of the most distracting things on a visit was when they had a mirror on the opposite wall, so I had to look into it while we were talking. I couldn't help looking at myself! I would notice if my hair wasn't combed or my tie wasn't straight. Sometimes, it would become so distracting that I had to change chairs to avoid seeing myself.

That happens often when we are trying to help or listen to others. Instead of noticing them, we think about what *they* see in *us*. As a result, we do not hear them. We are trapped in thoughts of ourselves, even when we ought to be thinking of others.

Sometimes we need to change our seat in the conversation. Being obsessed with our feelings, even if it is the feeling of being an inadequate listener, means we are not paying attention to others.

Vainglory makes a mirror out of everyone we see, and we become obsessed over how they see us rather than how we see them. When free of vainglory, we do not think of ourselves at all.

Empathy—the opposite of vainglory

Empathy is connecting with the feelings of others. Their feelings become our feelings. Empathy is what we mean when we say "intimacy." We empathically connect with God through prayer, and He connects empathically with us. God sends us empathic feelings that draw us close to Him or push us away from undesirable things. Empathy is how the Holy Spirit draws us to the Word and to worship.

Empathy comes when we care about the feelings of others. When we have empathy with another, we start caring about how they feel and stop worrying about how they make us feel. Empathy draws us out of ourselves into the soul of another person.

People who look to others to see themselves miss the beauty of other souls. Instead, they are only mirrors we look into to see our reflection.

Imagine walking through a forest on a clear, calm day when you come across a still pool of water. You stare into the pool, and your reflection is the first thing you see. This is what vainglory is like. In every person you meet, you see your reflection. Now, look a little deeper in the pool. Suddenly, you become aware that a new world of fish, plants, and other aquatic life is under the surface. You don't see it at first because you are staring at yourself, but you see wonderful things once you look beyond yourself.

Everyone we meet is like that reflective pool. If we can stop worrying about how we look at them, we can see the wonders that each person brings us. Empathy frees us from looking for love and assurance from others. It enables us to look at them as they are, not what they are in our relationships with others. Every human is a deep ocean; great ideas and emotions can be found underneath the surface. Empathy is our ability to stare at others in wonder.

Empathy enables us to love our enemies since we are not judging them by how they judge us. We can recognize something of God in everyone we see and in every situation presented to us. The world ceases to be about ourselves and becomes full of excitement as we feel the feelings of others.

Empathy erases our self-consciousness and replaces it with God and other consciousness, which is the essence of enjoyment. We can see the world as a playground, not a prison. People become books to read, each exciting in itself.

Fellowship is shared empathy. We no longer are "you" and "I" but "us." We feel the same and recognize each other's feelings. This is the opposite of vainglory, where we stay aware of ourselves even when together. *Koinonia* is losing ourselves in each other, while we both lose ourselves in God. We can only do this when we are free from vainglory. Otherwise, everything is just a mirror. But when we can open ourselves up to others, each person becomes a gateway to a more beautiful world.

Second Rank--The "Sign" Cancers

Anger

My dear brothers and sisters, take note of this: Everyone should be quick to listen, slow to speak, and slow to become angry because human anger does not produce the righteousness that God desires. Therefore, get rid of all moral filth and the evil that is so prevalent, and humbly accept the word planted in you, which can save you. James 1: 19-21

Anger is the first of the second group of soul cancers. These bad thoughts help us to know when other bad thoughts are around. Evagrius compares these bad thoughts to a mean dog chained to a homeowner's porch. When you see the dog, you know the homeowner is warning you to stay away. We can then assume that something valuable is hidden inside that he does not want you to see. If we get angry for no reason, we should look deeper to see what we are hiding from ourselves.

Anger isn't always bad. God Himself gets angry. The phrases "Wrath of God" and "God's wrath" appear thirty-three times in the King James Version, 48 times in the New International Version, and 50 times in the English Standard Version of the Bible.

Jesus got angry, too. I once read through the Gospels and marked every time Jesus became angry. I had marks on almost every page. He called the Scribes and Pharisees hypocrites, ran the money changers out of the temple, and even got angry with his disciples when they were slow to get His point. If God and Jesus get angry, people created in God's image must also get angry sometimes.

In Ephesians 4:26, Paul wrote, *"Be angry, but do not sin."* Paul lost his temper sometimes, but usually for righteous and justifiable reasons. It's clear in the Bible that anyone who follows Jesus will sometimes get angry, too.

We are hardwired to get angry at injustice. We need appropriate anger to stand up against abuse and neglect. Without the extra blast of adrenalin, we might be tempted to let it go unaddressed. Sometimes, we need our anger to change ourselves and the world.

But wrath isn't the same as anger. Wrath is anger when it spreads that is misdirected and abused. Wrath is anger when it becomes a soul cancer. It stores up inside of us, like static electricity. We strike out at whoever or whatever is nearby when it grows too strong. Wrath is anger that grows beyond its bounds. We yell at someone and hit them when only a mild rebuke is needed. Wrath isn't about good or bad, right or wrong. It is an ugly thing that hurts everyone around us.

Anger has a purpose; wrath does not. Anger is specific at a particular target; wrath strikes whatever is near. Anger is a bullet; wrath is a bomb. Anger has a reason; wrath has none. Anger corrects; wrath destroys.

We might feel anger if someone cuts us off in traffic, but we forget it quickly. Wrath wants us to swear undying vengeance against them. Evagrius called this feeling *irascibility*—a general grumpiness towards everyone and everything. If we feel this general grumpiness, we should take it as a warning and seek the reason why. Once we find what makes us angry, we should give those reasons to God.

Wrath shows us something is wrong. Let's take Bill, for example. Bill drinks three cups of coffee a day. He's a caffeine addict, but he doesn't know it. Without telling him, his wife substitutes decaffeinated coffee for his regular caffeine. Bill gets irritated and barks at people all day. He realizes his behavior isn't normal for him. When he finds out what his wife did, he realizes he is addicted. He recognizes his addiction and vows to cut back. After a few days of drinking less coffee, his irritation goes away. His wrath was a signal to him that something else was wrong.

Disproportionate anger is also a warning sign. Let's say someone bumps into you in a crowd. Usually, it wouldn't bother you. But if you are already stressed, you might snarl at them or push back. This is not an appropriate response. It is a signal that there is something else in your life that is stressing you. You need to deal with that hidden anger to avoid taking it out on others.

It's hard to admit when we are angry, even to ourselves. But there is no way of getting rid of wrath unless we admit it exists first. We must admit to the buried source of our wrath if we want to stop getting angry at everything.

The Effects of Wrath

Of all the soul cancers, anger is the most contagious. Epidemiologist Stephen Leeder argues that anger spreads just like an infectious disease.[6] When one person explodes in violence, it draws out the anger of others. *"He who lives by the sword dies by the sword,"* Jesus said. A general atmosphere of violence spreads when one person reacts violently. That is why Jesus told us to stop violence whenever possible. *"Whoever strikes you on one cheek, turn the other to them also."* We must keep our temper on a tight leash, or it will spread to everyone around us.

---

[6]Stephen Leeder, "Epidemiology in an age of Anger and Complaint," *International Journal of Epidemiology*, Volume 46, Issue 1, February 2017, Page . https://doi.org/10.1093/ije/dyx009

We should know the warning signs of anger so that we can stop when we see them in ourselves. They include:

- Physical sensations such as quickened breath, dry mouth, or jitteriness.
- Taking offense at small slights.
- Raised or quickened voice.
- Categorizing everyone into "good" and "bad" people.
- Excusing sins in ourselves that we condemn in others.

When these characteristics are present, we need to stop and get hold of ourselves before we say another word. Our wrath is of no use to ourselves or God.

Forgiveness—the opposite of anger

Forgiveness is choosing to let go of an argument. It is not a cure for anger, but it is a necessary step in learning to live with it.

Forgiveness is strong medicine in any broken relationship. When we let go of a slight or an annoyance, it is easier for others to let go of ours. Forgiveness focuses our attention on God instead of dwelling on others' faults. It also stops the roots of bitterness from spreading to other parts of our lives.

God's forgiveness is the basis for all human society. The only reason we have life and breath is that God forgave us. Human society, therefore, rests on the truth that God withholds his wrath from sinners. One day, patience will run out, and the world will shake.

Since God is forgiving, it makes sense that forgiveness would be expected of us towards others. In Matthew 18, Jesus told the parable of the unmerciful servant. A servant who owed a tremendous amount to his master refused to forgive a small amount owed to him by another servant. When the master heard about it, he had the unmerciful servant thrown into prison. Jesus said, *"This is how my heavenly Father will treat each of you unless you forgive your brother or sister from your heart."* (Matthew 18:35). Jesus said in the Sermon on the Mount, *"Forgive us our debts, as we forgive our debtors."* Then He said, *"For if you do not forgive others their trespasses, neither will your Heavenly Father forgive you."* God is serious about forgiveness.

Forgiveness isn't so much a requirement, though, as a road to liberation. Resentment against a person acts like handcuffs, holding us to them for life. We cannot be free of them until we let go of resentment. Forgiveness is the key that unlocks the cuffs. Letting go of hurt means we can let go of people who have hurt us.

Forgiveness is always a process. It begins with not seeking revenge, progresses to verbally declaring them forgiven, and finally moves on to emotional healing of the relationship. We often get stuck in that process.

Forgiveness is often misunderstood. It does not mean we feel all right about a person who hurt us. It merely means that we give up any right for restitution or vengeance. When we are angry at someone, we feel they owe us a debt. Forgiveness is simply canceling that debt.

What about large hurts like abuse, neglect, or criminal activities? We must be much more careful here. We cannot hide serious harm under forgiveness and expect it to disappear. We must know the difference between *forgiveness* and *reconciliation*.

Forgiveness is needed first for our protection and well-being, not just for the person who offended us. When deeply hurt, we forgive for our own sake to break the chains of our anger that control us. By foregoing vengeance and restitution, we break their tie to us. We do this for our own sake; we simply realize that seeking revenge or restitution will cost us more than the offense is worth.

I remember a man I knew whose wife divorced him, claiming he was abusive. Whether he was or not, I couldn't say. After the divorce, he dedicated himself to clearing his name by bringing her to court and to church discipline to prove himself right and her wrong. In the end, he proved nothing. He wasted years in a futile search for justice. If he had let it go—in other words, *forgiven*—he might not have wasted years of time and effort.

A harder situation arises when we are talking about violent, abusive, or criminal people. We may forgive, but we must be careful about reconciliation. Forgiveness may be immediate, but reconciliation is much harder and more complicated. Abusers will often look at their victims and demand that we forgive them as Christians, treating them as if the offense did not happen. But this is just a ruse to entrap us in an abusive relationship, keeping them free to do it again.

Christians have been taught to forgive, but they are never told to continue in an abusive relationship. Forgiveness without change does not set either the abuser or his victim free but just keeps them both in bondage. Do not reconcile with an abuser or criminal until steps have been taken to ensure there will be no more abuse. Only then, after the abuser has taken steps to change his ways, should real reconciliation be attempted.

After abuse, residual anger stays around, even when we have given them to God. But God gives us the strength to overcome our feelings.

Bishop Desmond Tutu was a South African leader who was the victim of apartheid, the system of white supremacy that plagued his country for generations. When apartheid ended, many former government members expected they would be imprisoned or executed for their crimes against blacks. Instead, Bishop Tutu organized courts of reconciliation, where anyone who would confess their sins against blacks would be forgiven and set free, officially forgiven.

Bishop Tutu was asked how he could forgive and love those who hurt him during these courts. He replied that he had not personally reconciled. He still felt anger over the harm they had caused. However, through God's grace, he found the strength to ignore his feelings and not seek revenge. Anger did not rule him, even though he still prayed it would go away one day.

Reconciliation is always possible when we behave lovingly toward those who have hurt us. The emotions follow later, as the Spirit of God works healing in our souls. Even the biggest wounds can be healed through Christ's forgiveness over time.

Elizabeth Eliot writes in her book *Through the Gates of Splendor* about her husband, Jim. He was one of five missionaries murdered by members of the Auca tribe in South America when they went there to spread the Gospel.

After hearing of her husband's death and mourning her husband, Elizabeth went to the Aucas and completed her husband's mission. She shared the Gospel and saw them converted. Years later, she appeared at the World Conference on Evangelism in Switzerland with one of the tribal leaders. She introduced him as her spiritual brother, father, and dear friend. Then she added, "He was also the man who killed my husband." Her forgiveness and reconciliation came naturally through the power of the Holy Spirit.

Anger starts good, as all things do. But when it becomes cancer, it can poison our lives. Only through God's forgiveness can anger be removed from our hearts.

Shame

"And hope does not put us to shame because God's love has been poured into our hearts through the Holy Spirit, who has been given to us." Romans 5:5

Have you ever done something that made you want to hit yourself on the forehead and say, "I can't believe I was that stupid"? That feeling of self-anger is a *shame*. Shame is a warning that tells us we have or are about to do something wrong. Shame is good for us because it reminds us to change our ways. It is a necessary part of our emotional makeup.

Good shame leads us to see our sins as God sees them. The word "confess" means literally "to agree with." When we confess our sins, we agree with God that our sinful behavior is wrong. Confession is a thought that recognizes something is wrong; a feeling, since we hurt when we realize we have hurt God; and an action, since it involves restitution for what we have done wrong and changing what we will do.

Shame is good, but it should also be temporary. When we have declared that we are wrong and our apology has been accepted., that should be the end of the matter. If it hangs around afterward, then it becomes soul cancer.

Shame isn't always our fault. Sometimes, shame is imposed on us from how others see us. If a person is violated or abused, they often feel guilty, but that guilt is unjustified. This does not come from our sins but from the sins of others projected on us. We cannot repent this shame because we have done nothing to repent. This is a false shame, an illusion created by a shameless society. But even so, a false shame can feel like a real shame. To be free, though, we must rid ourselves of shame that does not come from God. In that case, it is much harder to recover. This usually takes a long time and the help of friends and counselors.

Shame should not be confused with guilt. Guilt is a moral state of being outside of God's will, which will harm God's reputation, ourselves, or others. But there are many people.

Shame can dominate our lives. If shame persists too long, it becomes free-floating. It is no longer helpful but makes us feel that everything we say or do is wrong. Shame must come from actual sin to have any good use.

Our shame should be proportionate to our offense. If we feel great shame for minor or slight shame for great sins, we do not see ourselves as God sees us. The same shame for all is counterproductive if we always have the same amount of shame. What's the point of confessing major sins if I feel just as ashamed for doing minor ones? Overeating at meals should produce guilt, but not as much as stealing a car. If we have too much shame, we accept it as usual and give up trying to improve. Shamelessness is helpful to those who know what it is to be innocent but useless to those who don't know anything but guilt.

The Apostle John tells us how to get rid of shame in 1 John 1:9. "*If we confess our sins, he is faithful and just to forgive our sins, and cleanse us from all unrighteousness(shame).*" First, we admit we have sinned. This is more than lip service; it also means allowing ourselves to experience shame for what we have done. Confession without shame is not likely to change our lives.

Confession of sin should be specific. We should not simply say, "God, I'm a sinner." We should get specific. "God, I mistreated my wife," or "God, I stole pencils from work." Name what we have done wrong. A casual, non-specific confession does us a little good.

Freedom from shame requires restitution when possible. Shame leads us to make substantial efforts to avoid certain behaviors. Shame is the fire alarm that goes off whenever we have offended our conscience. It stops ringing when we have confessed and repented.

The more we live in holiness and forgiveness, the more we become sensitive to shame. But healthy guilt is not overwhelming because we recognize that we are terrible people, loved by a wonderful God. Although we commit sins often, we can deal with them and give them to God so they will not grow larger. Good shame helps us notice our sins before they grow and root them out.

Cancerous shame is not like this. It becomes a cloud, a dark companion, that hangs close to us, keeping us from seeing our worth before God. When shame becomes a cancer, it is no longer a symptom of something wrong but a disease that destroys. It attaches itself to things that are not shameful, making us apologize for everything we do, good or bad. It becomes larger than the sins we have committed. Every little failure becomes enormous. We demand perfection from ourselves and are no good if we don't accomplish it. Good shame leads us to become good people and leads us to God. Bad shame leads us to think we are nothing but evil until all we are left with is hopelessness. Shame is like a fire alarm. What would happen if your fire alarm rang all the time? Eventually, you would grow used to it. If you did have a fire, it would be of no help. Shame has to be occasional, or else it is just a nuisance.

But when we confess our sins, our sense of shame dissipates as quickly as it comes. The purpose of shame is to lead us to the Cross. Christ died to erase the feeling of shame by covering it with His Blood. *"For God commended His love to us, that while we were still sinners, Christ died for us."* (Romans 5:8)

Sadly, shame often comes to us, even when we have done nothing wrong. Other people, often parents or other authority figures, think shaming us will make us do better in life. Instead of unconditional love, they give us an unhealthy dose of shame. They fuss at us about everything we do. This shaming is usually for selfish motives, to make us into their image instead of God's. Abusive authorities shift the focus of their sins onto us until we believe we are terrible, unlovable people.

Let's use an example. Cathy grew up in a shame-based household. Her parents were beautiful, successful people who expected her to be the same. Her hair was never combed well enough for her mother. His mother always told her she should lose a few pounds until Cathy believed her best efforts were insufficient. Her high grades were never perfect. Her father fussed at her that she was always too loud, too flighty, or too careless. Cathy grew up believing she was never as good as she could be. This feeling was reinforced at church, where the preachers always taught moralistic sermons about how to be better, love more, witness more, and be holier. If you didn't feel guilty every Sunday, you hadn't been listening. Little was said about the unconditional love God has for us. Cathy felt that God may love her, but He didn't like her.

Should a parent ever scold a child, a wife scold a husband, or a preacher scold a congregation? Of course—sometimes! But scolding should be short, and praise should be long. The only purpose for scolding is to make us better people. When the point is made, then the praise should start. Scolding should never be used as a kind of punishment, and punishment should only be used when necessary.

There are two wrong ways of dealing with shame. The first is *perfectionism.* If only we can behave perfectly, we think the shame will disappear. This can't work, though, because something about us always needs improvement. Only God is perfect, and we are not God. The best we can hope for is to be a better person than yesterday. We will never be perfect.

The other wrong way is *denial.* We tell ourselves, "I am a good person, so I have done nothing to be ashamed of." This doesn't work because we are *not* perfect, even if we pretend to be. Any sensible person will notice things in themselves they don't like. To maintain the fiction of perfection, we must lie to ourselves and become hypocrites. Some people deny their shame by excusing themselves for what they despise in others or lowering their lower standards until there are none left. We may look for people worse than ourselves and condemn them so that we can feel better. I once read about a father whose son was arrested for stealing cars. The father defended his son to the police, saying, "Sure, my son steals cars, but he never stripped on in his life. No way!"

Another way we deal with our shame is by projecting it onto others. We blame others for our problems—parents, society, racism, advertisements, Democrats, Republicans, Communists, etc. We see ourselves as victims, not sinners. We turn off the fire alarm against sin and sleep through the fire in blissful ignorance.

Shame is like a fire alarm. It goes off when we do something wrong, so we will know how to react. But if the fire alarm is always clanging, we will learn to ignore it. We must answer the call to fix what is wrong or risk losing our moral sense altogether.

If we confess our sins to God, shame goes away. But if shame doesn't result in repentance, it hangs around forever. Good shame gives way to joy. Bad shame stays with us forever.

Gratitude—the angel against Shame

We all understand that we must repent if we sin and are ashamed of our actions. But repentance is often misunderstood. The Greek word for repentance is *metanoia*, which means "to change our minds." Richard Rohr defines *metanoia* as putting on a new thought or attitude to see the world differently. Repentance is like putting on new glasses.

When we live in constant shame, we must change our minds and see God and the world differently. If we see God constantly through the eyes of shame, then He becomes the "criticizer in chief." All we see of God is His judgment. But if we put on new glasses and see God first as a God of love, we realize His blessings are everywhere. Every breath, every morsel of food, every outburst of laughter or ray of sunshine comes from a God who loves us. All the good things of earth have been given to us despite our sins, not as a reward for good behavior.

God does not expect us to be perfect, but He loves us as we are. His attitude towards us is not based on the sins we committed but on His ability to forgive all our sins. He has already justified our sins to Him through the cross, so we don't have to think about them.

When we put on the glasses of gratitude, we look at everything differently. We are suddenly able to see good things in every circumstance and situation in life.

Let's say you have an electric bill you cannot pay. A friend of yours promises to pay your electric bill. You are very appreciative, but how do you thank him? Please don't bother baking him a cake or sending him a thank-you card. The first way to thank him is by enjoying the electricity he just paid for! We live in our forgiveness instead of wallowing in our sins.

Gratitude is also being thankful for the good things you are doing. Before you kick yourself for your mistakes, give thanks for what you have gotten right. You will find there is more to be grateful for than ashamed.

Sometimes, we can be terrible sinners. Even so, God loves us as we are. There is no need to be ashamed when seeing God's acceptance of us. We do not have to feel ashamed when forgiven for our sins. We don't need to focus on the negative, but we can be thankful for God's forgiveness.

In our church, when we take the Lord's supper, the pastor pronounces these words-- "This is the feast of victory for our God!" Every time God forgives us, it is a new victory. Whenever we enjoy eating ice cream, seeing a baby, smelling a flower, or seeing a sunset, it is a sign of God's favor on us despite our problems and sins. We do not need to look back on past wounds, but we can focus forward with gratitude for what God has given us and will give us in the future.

Part 3: The Final Rank--Fear, Nostalgia, Despair, Pride

Fear

Fear not, for I am with you; be not dismayed, for I am your God. I will strengthen you, help you; I will uphold you with my righteous right hand." Isaiah 41:10

On a chess board, the back row of pieces is the strongest. This is true with soul cancers, too. The last four—fear, nostalgia (or grief), despair, and especially pride are the hardest to recognize and conquer. Yet, if we can learn to overcome them, nothing becomes impossible for us.

Fear is perhaps the most obvious of the four. Fear is not bad in itself. Fear, in its proper place, is good. We read in Proverbs 1:7, *"The fear of the Lord is the beginning of knowledge."* But we also read in 2 Timothy 1:7, *"God has not given us a spirit of fear but of power and love and a sound mind."* Hebrews 13:6 says, *"The Lord is my helper. I will not fear."* But Psalm 33:18 says, *"The eye of the Lord is on those who fear Him."* So, does God want us to fear or not?

We ought to be afraid sometimes. Fear is a part of love. Any happily married man will both love and fear their wife. We are afraid of hurting or disappointing those we love. We love our children and fear not being good fathers or mothers. We fear failing to serve the people we love properly.

Christians feel this way about God. We don't want to disappoint Him in any way. This fear keeps us striving to be better servants and lovers of Him.

Good fear is a gift from God to help protect us. Fear triggers the "fight or flight" response—we either run away from danger or fight against it. Once the threat is gone, the fear leaves, too.

Sometimes, fear does not leave us but lingers like an unwanted guest. We can tell good fear from bad in several ways.

Good fear is about something specific. Bad fears are not. How do you eliminate a fear about something you can't see or know?

Good fear is temporary. Bad fears are permanent. We never get rid of anxiety because we cannot know what it is. Fighting anxiety is like fighting a ghost.

Good fear leads us to action. Bad fears cannot be acted upon. We might fear meteors, but we can do nothing about it. The emotion of fear rises inside as if we can take some action, but we are helpless to do anything.

Good fear is love-based. Bad fears are loss-based. We do not have to fear our losses because we know God will protect and give us everything. But if we do not believe in God, there is nothing to do but fear everything since we cannot control the universe. Nothing will make us happy. If we lose God, fear is everywhere.

Anxiety

Bad fear is what we call *anxiety*. Anxiety is our reaction to a non-specific threat. Unlike good fear that is temporary, anxiety over our troubles hangs on like the stench of cigarettes after the smoker is gone. Our body reacts to anxiety as it reacts to fear—adrenalin goes up, muscles tense, heart races, etc. When we are anxious, the body wearies of that adrenalin push, and we become tired, nervous, and on edge. Anxiety dominates our lives, and we become prisoners of our fear.

The Old Testament gives us an example of bad fear in Proverbs 22:13: *"The sluggard says, 'There is a lion outside! I shall be killed in the streets!'"* This short verse tells us three important facts about this man. First, he doesn't know if a lion is in the streets because he hasn't been out to look for himself. He just heard about it through rumor. Today, we hear scary things on the news and somehow think that something happening half a world away is an immediate danger at our home. He has become closeted due to fear and only knows what he is told.

Second, if there *is* a lion in the street, it is still God's lion. Danger always exists, but God is always in control. We do not have to fear anything for long when we believe in God's protection.

Jesus told the story of a man who stored grain in barns. He took every precaution not to starve, yet he died that night. No amount of cowering inside or hiring protection will ever keep harm away, and no foe can ever harm us as long as God is with us. Our anxiety does not make us any safer. God determines whether we live or die; nothing can keep us completely safe.

Third, notice what the writer of Proverbs calls the person in the house—a *sluggard* or lazy. We usually think of a lazy person as someone who loves the pleasure of rest too much. But this person has become a sluggard because he has not stood up to his fear enough to take an acceptable risk. "Better safe than sorry" is good advice sometimes, but sometimes it is better to risk being sorry than staying safe. If our life were completely without risk, it would also be dull and unproductive. Risk is present in every situation.

The hardest battles we ever fight are our inner ones against soul cancers, especially our fears. If we adopt the motto, as many do, "better safe than sorry," we should realize that nothing will make us sorrier than choosing safety over life.

When I was a child, I took swimming lessons. The scariest part was jumping off the high dive. I got in line and climbed the ladder, but I froze when I got to the top and saw how high it was. I can still hear the laughter of the other children as I crawled past them down that ladder. I was greatly embarrassed. Later, I could face my fears and climb up the high dive again, and to my surprise, I enjoyed it. I could have avoided embarrassment if I had ignored my anxiety. We always lose something of ourselves when we listen to our fears to the exclusion of everything else.

Another example of this principle is the "parable of the talents" in Matthew 25: 14-30. In Jesus' story, three servants are given five, two, and one talent of gold by their master. Each servant was to return the money when the master returned, plus whatever interest the money had earned. When the master returned, the servant with five talents returned it all and five more talents to his master. Likewise, the second servant returned two talents, with two more from interest. The third servant, who had one talent, still only had one talent. The master was angry with him because he had no interest in the investment. The servant replied to the master that he knew the master was a hard man, and he was afraid that he might lose the money if he did invest it, so he buried the talent in the ground.

The master yelled at the servant, *"You wicked, lazy servant!"* Notice the word lazy here. *"So, you knew that I harvest where I have not sown and gather where I have not scattered seed? Well then, you should have deposited my money with the bankers so that I would have received it back with interest when I returned.* "Again, laziness is associated with being anxious. There was nothing wrong with feeling fear, but acting on fear when we should move forward is laziness. He was lazy because he surrendered to anxiety instead of fighting it. As a result, he lost it all.

When we are anxious, we all act in different ways. One way is to withdraw into our rooms and avoid life. Another way is to have a panic attack. Panic attacks have physical symptoms—dry mouth, sweat, feelings of chills, chest pains, etc.

But these physical symptoms are nothing compared to the spiritual problems it causes. Anxiety steals our trust in God. We forget our Creator and His ability to rescue us. Not until the panic attack is over can we see the beauty and bounty of His love.

Fear has a place in us, but that place is not in the driver's seat. Fear can keep us out of trouble as a wary backseat passenger, but if it gains control, it will never let go.

Controlling Anxiety

I have a list of useless statements that people say to each other. They include "Don't take this personally," "Stop worrying," and "Be careful." I have never known anyone who stopped worrying because someone told them to or a teenager who ever behaved more responsibly simply because their parents told them to be careful. These kinds of statements are usually a waste of breath.

But when we explain why we should not be anxious, it can help a lot. For example, in Philippians 4 6, Paul says, *"be anxious over nothing." Still,"* he then adds, *"in everything by prayer and supplication with thanksgiving, let your requests be made known to God."* Don't be anxious because God will give you what you need. Philippians 4:10 says, *"I can do everything through Christ, who strengthens me."* Verse 19, *"For my God will supply all your needs according to His riches in Christ Jesus."* Don't be anxious; God will give you what you need to survive.

Don't try to fight anxiety—you'll lose. Instead, look to God, and He will give you strength.

Another way to fight anxiety is to clarify your priorities. Discover what's important. Another way of saying this is to discover what you really love. Anxiety is usually worrying about losing someone or something we love. So, do we really love riches so much that we fear losing them? Does what people think of us matter so much to us? If we put God first, those things are unimportant. We need to ask God to change our lives and priorities to face the loss of all things without fear.

Freedom doesn't come from owning a lot but from needing little. I easily give away things I do not need but keep what I need or love. But I do not need to be anxious when God gives me everything.

Courage—fear's corresponding virtue

Anxiety never goes completely away because it, too, has a purpose. We all face uncertainty about the future. Unspecific fears are common to us all. Therefore, we cannot say that our goal is to be always calm. It is the anxiety that leads us to panic that we really must fear. Panic is having such anxiety that we either become paralyzed, unable to function, or run away in the face of danger.

The opposite of anxiety isn't calm; it's *courage*. Courage isn't the absence of fear.
In fact, it's impossible to have courage without fear. Courage is the ability to live with fear but not in fear. Fear exists in us, but it does not control our lives.

Courage can only be found in weak and frightened people. Only those who are scared can have courage. In *The Lord of the Rings*, there's a beautiful scene where the hero, Aragorn, leads troops into battle against the forces of ultimate evil. He tells them, "I see in your eyes the same fear that would also take my heart—but not today!" Before conquering the enemy, they must first conquer their fear. This is courage: to be afraid but not act upon it.

There are four stages to courage. First, we must *love something enough to give our life for it.* Just as love is impossible without fear, courage is impossible without love. When called upon to have courage, we must be clear about what we love. We don't go into battle for a country we don't love or risk martyrdom for a faith we don't have. Love must come before courage.

Second, we must *simplify our priorities by making choices.* The prophet Elijah told the Israelites, "How long will you hop between branches. If God be God, serve Him. If Baal be god, follow him." (I Kings 18:21). We can't follow two ways at once. We are called upon to stand up for our beliefs, and when we think that our stand might cost us our lives or our families, we hesitate. It is important to simplify our love before the crisis comes. We must find our greatest love and cling to it, no matter what dangers we face.

When courageous people face danger, they do not make a choice. They realize that they have already chosen. When he joins the army, a soldier gives his life for his country. A married man does not choose to be faithful to his wife every day. He did it when they got engaged. Christ chose the world over His comfort in heaven. Paul chose celibacy and persecution over the life of an affluent Jewish leader. We all have to choose. For a Christian to "take up his cross" means that we have made a choice—death in this world for life in the next.

C S. Lewis wrote. "Submit to death, death of your ambitions and favorite wishes every day and death of your whole body in the end: submit with every fiber of your being, and you will find eternal life."[7]

Third, we must *pray to God for the strength to act*. We have no hope when infected with the soul cancer of fear. We must have God's help to overcome it. It does no good to tell a panicked person to fight the panic. God must give them calm. There is great power in prayer, not just because God answers it, but because we have already given up control when we pray. Praying for strength acknowledges that our strength is not enough. God is bigger than our fears and stronger than our panic.

Finally, we should *thank God as He takes control*. Once we have surrendered control to Him, we can act according to His will. It does not matter if we win or lose; the only thing that matters is that God is in control.

There's an adage that we should live in a way that, when we come to the end of our lives, we will not discover that we never really lived. The soul cancer of fear prevents us from going after our best life. Ultimately, it will leave us with an empty bag of memories, having done nothing challenging or important, without scars or medals. But when we live with courage, we may hurt or even be crushed. Even so, we will have lived, which is much better than the alternative.

---

[7] C. S. Lewis, Mere Christianity,

Nostalgia (Grief)

Brothers and sisters, I do not consider myself yet to have taken hold of it. But one thing I do: Forgetting what is behind and straining toward what is ahead, 1 press on toward the goal to win the prize for which God has called me heavenward in Christ Jesus. Philippians 3:13

Mark Twain once told a story about a little girl whose family was packing a wagon to move to Missouri. She walks around the farm, saying goodbye to all her favorite things— "Goodbye, house, I'm going to Missouri. Goodbye trees, I'm going to Missouri. Goodbye brook, I'm going to Missouri. Goodbye God, I'm going to Missouri."

Then he stops and corrects himself about the last statement. "No, that's not how she said it--what she said was, '*Good*, by God, I'm going to Missouri!"

This story shows both the good and bad sides of grief. When we move, we mourn the loss of our old connections and friendships. Eventually, though, we get over it and go on living. We can't grieve forever; we must all move on.

"Good" Grief

Grief is the "flip side" of love. If we enjoy someone or something, we feel sad when it is taken away. Not taking the time to grieve can harm our body and soul. If we don't deal with our griefs, they pile up, one upon another, until we eventually break down.

Grief is necessary, but it should be temporary. Tears help us to work out our grief and move on. Jesus tells us in John 16:20,

"Very truly I tell you, you will weep and mourn while the world rejoices. You will grieve, but your grief will turn to joy." Grieving helps us put away our pain so that we can live again.

It's not just the loss of people or things that we grieve, but our own failures, too. Grief and shame are connected. Acknowledging our failures and grieving them helps us come closer to God. Denying or not facing our sins and failures pushes us farther away from Him.

We all need tears of grief and repentance in our lives from time to time. Tears do not make us weaker. They make us stronger.

Bad grief

Evagrius spoke of bad grief as having a different name—*nostalgia*. When we use that word today, we usually think of it as loving the past. But it actually means a *sickness* for the past. It originally meant becoming stuck in a previous time because we did not want to live in the present.

Nostalgia can take many forms, but these three manifestations are the most common.

The first kind of nostalgia is the grief that *never resolves*. Any grief goes away slowly. One minute, we think we're better; the next moment, we are plunged back into the depths again. But over time, as we work on our grief through tears and talking, the power of grief diminishes. The intervals between our crying fits grow longer, and there is time for other feelings to surface. In time, we can think back on what we have lost without being filled with sadness.

In nostalgia, we become obsessed with thinking about the past until we believe there is nothing to look forward to. We hang on to yesterday and refuse to acknowledge today.

The second kind of nostalgia is *grieving about the wrong things.* Most pleasures were always supposed to be temporary. Suppose we become confused and believe that what was supposed to be temporary is actually permanent. In that case, we are setting ourselves up for grief.

A third kind of nostalgia is a *general longing for the "good old days."* There is nothing wrong with loving the past. Our memories help us to retain wisdom and stability. Memories can be a blessing to our imaginations, allowing us to revisit essential points in our development. But many live in the past because they find the present unbearable.

Nostalgia isn't how we view the past but how we live in the present. When we lose ourselves in grief, we miss God's new blessings in store for us.

Past sickness isn't only a sickness of the old. Young people get it, too, when they refuse to face adulthood. In fact, senior citizens may have an advantage over the young in avoiding past-sickness because they have already seen many changes. When facing their first changes in life, young people can be more uncomfortable than older people who have already learned to adapt to constant change.

Nostalgia can turn us into hoarders. We do not love antiques for their own sake but only as reminders of our childhood. Grandmother's teacup, Father's watch, or an old business sign from the family business have enormous sentimental value to us, so much that we can't bear to part with them, even when they break beyond repair. But our memories are in our hearts, not our shelves. Objects are unnecessary to help us remember what is really important to us.

Living in a fantasy world

Fantasy is a soul cancer closely related to grief. Just as some people run to the past, to a world that used to be, others run to worlds that never were, to fiction and fantasy.

This is not a condemnation of fiction of any kind. Fictional stories can sometimes be more true than real ones. The morality of stories like *Lord of the Rings* or *The Chronicles of Narnia* can challenge and inspire us, and so can the best of science fiction and fantasy. But the problem comes when fiction becomes a substitute for real life. Jesus used fictional parables to make important points about the world. But when the world becomes too frightening or hard, fantasy can be a temptation to escape our problems instead of a way of solving them. The real world is scary sometimes. But it is also more beautiful than any fantasy can be. We must live in the present, not escape into the past or future.

Nostalgia is not logical. It is a feeling when we are disappointed with our current situation. The only way to counteract it is to find joy in the present.

The Angel of joy

How do we escape from escapism? By finding joy in the present.

A college student loses his homesickness when he starts enjoying college life. A little girl who moves to Missouri discovers things to like about the trip. We still miss home but find new friends and new songs. A widow always misses her husband but finds new joys in living. *"Weeping may tarry for the night, but joy comes in the morning."* Psalm 30:5.

The Book of Lamentations is probably the Bible's most miserable, depressing book. It is a funeral dirge sung by the prophet Jeremiah over the destruction of Jerusalem. Jeremiah has seen his beloved city, his relatives, and his entire way of life destroyed by the Babylonians. Lamentations express his true feelings of sorrow and sadness.

Even so, there is joy in it. Consider his words in Lamentations 3:19-24:

> *I remember my affliction and my wandering, the bitterness, and the gall.*
> *I well remember them, and my soul is downcast within me.*
> *Yet this I call to mind and therefore I have hope:*
> *Because of the LORD's great love, we are not consumed, for his compassions never fail.*
> *They are new every morning; great is your faithfulness.*
> *I say to myself, "The LORD is my portion; therefore I will wait for him."*

We must grieve, but we don't have to wallow in it. God sends us fresh things to enjoy every day. Sunrises are still beautiful. Children still laugh. Flowers still smell sweet. Little blessings are everywhere, even in the hardest times.

The celebration of life should be there, even while we are mourning a death. Take every opportunity to celebrate the joys around you. Grief is strong, but it does not give us strength. Joy is necessary to give us the strength to go on with life. The closer we draw to God, the more He gives us joy.

Spiritual progression is not about giving things up. It is about earning new joys. When we are young and happy, we might say that it can never get better than it is. Then God surprises us with new joys, and we suddenly realize that life can get better and has! Along the way, some blessings leave us, but for everyone we leave behind, two open before us, if only we have the eyes to see them. The more we celebrate God's gifts in our lives, the greater our joy, and the less we need to cling to the past.

Apathy (Despair)

Whatever your hand finds to do, do it with all your
might, for in the realm of the dead, where you are going, there
is neither working nor planning nor knowledge nor wisdom.
Ecclesiastes 9:10

The desert monks called apathy the "noonday demon." That was because they only ate one meal daily, usually in the morning, but they worked all day in the fields. By noontime, they were already tired and hungry. They felt as if the work would never end. At noon, Satan began planting the seeds of despair inside them. By noon, they were sorely tempted to give up and go home.

"Apathy" is not broad enough to express what happens when the noonday demon calls. It can also be translated as *despair, laziness, sloth, depression, listlessness, boredom, apathy, and restlessness.* The word *Despair* probably comes closest to defining Apathy--a sense of hopelessness. *Apathy* is the notion that life will never get any better. It's like getting a fortune cookie that says, "Today is the last best day of your life, and it's all downhill from here." Apathy is pessimism on steroids—nothing in front of you but the 'same old thing."

C. S. Lewis described this best in *The Screwtape Letters.*

"Humans are amphibians—half spirit and half animal.
(The Enemy's determination to produce such a revolting
hybrid was one of the things that determined Our Father to
withdraw his support from Him.) As spirits, they belong to
the eternal world, but as animals, they inhabit time. This
means that while their spirit can be directed to an eternal

object, their bodies, passions, and imaginations are continually changing, for to be in time means to change. Therefore, their nearest approach to constancy is undulation—the repeated return to a level from which they repeatedly fall back, a series of troughs and peaks. If you had watched your patient carefully you would have seen this undulation in every department of his life—his interest in his work, his affection for his friends, his physical appetites, all go up and down. As long as he lives on earth periods of emotional and bodily richness and liveliness will alternate with periods of numbness and poverty. The dryness and dullness through which your patient is now going are not, as you fondly suppose, your workmanship; they are merely a natural phenomenon which will do us no good unless you make a good use of it."[8]

We all feel apathy sometimes. Hope usually stirs again, and we rediscover our sense of purpose. When the noonday demon hits, we slog through the boring stretches of life because we've developed good habits and perseverance. Despite our undulations of interest, we remember our higher purpose and choose to follow God more than the moment's mood.

But without purpose, or at least good habits, apathy can take possession of us.

In the seven deadly sins list, apathy is called "sloth" or "laziness." But apathy is much bigger than laziness. We think of a lazy person as someone addicted to rest. But apathy is not rest; it is not caring at all. Sometimes apathy means busying ourselves with distraction or pointless labor or jumping from one thing to

---

[8] Lewis, C. S.. The Screwtape Letters (pp. 37-38). HarperOne. Kindle Edition.

another to keep our minds off the fact that we have no purpose in anything we do.

In Lewis' book, The *Screwtape Letters*, He describes the Devil's goal in apathy.

> *"As this condition becomes more fully established, you will be gradually freed from the tiresome business of providing Pleasures as temptations. As the uneasiness and his reluctance to face it cut him off more and more from all real happiness, and as habit renders the pleasures of vanity and excitement and flippancy at once less pleasant and harder to forgo (for that is what habit fortunately does to a pleasure) you will find that anything or nothing is sufficient to attract his wandering attention. You no longer need a good book, which he really likes, to keep him from his prayers or his work or his sleep; a column of advertisements in yesterday's paper will do. You can make him waste his time not only in conversation he enjoys with people whom he likes but in conversations with those he cares nothing about on subjects that bore him. You can make him do nothing at all for long periods. You can keep him up late at night, not roistering, but staring at a dead fire in a cold room. All the healthy and out-going activities which we want him to avoid can be inhibited and nothing given in return, so that at least he may say, as one of my own patients said on his arrival down here, 'I now see that I spent most of my life in doing neither what I ought nor what I liked.' The Christians describe the Enemy as one 'without whom Nothing is strong'. And Nothing is very strong: strong enough to steal away a man's best years not in sweet sins but in a dreary flickering of the mind over it knows not what and knows not why, in the gratification of curiosities so feeble that the man is only half aware of them, in the drumming of fingers and kicking of*

heels, in whistling tunes that he does not like, or in the long,
dim labyrinth of reveries that have not even lust or ambition to
give them a relish, but which, once chance association has
started them, the creature is too weak and fuddled to shake
off."[9]

Apathy isn't just doing nothing. It can also be hyperactivity without purpose. Apathy can make us restless because we have no faith that our current path will lead anywhere worthwhile. We move from one job to another, one relationship to another, seeking excitement and stability. But every path we try seems as dull and pointless as the last one. We do not have the perseverance and resilience to see any goal through.

Apathy is a heart condition. It isn't dependent on the situation but a state of mind we have in all situations. We won't find hope just by changing jobs or spouses. Until we believe in hope, we are hopeless. The only way to get out of apathy is to start looking for hope in the ordinary, everyday places each day.

A life without hope leads to one logical end—suicide. By suicide, I do not mean a quick death by gun, pills, or rope, but the quiet, slow suicide of addictions and wasting time. Without hope, life becomes an endless quest to forget the future. It is suicide to give up and lay down, dulling our senses with hours of pointless entertainment until our bodies give up as our soul already has. Ultimately, we may discover that our life is nearly over, but we have never lived. Until we recover hope, nothing will ever satisfy us.

---

[9] Lewis, C. S. *The Screwtape Letters* (pp. 59-60). HarperOne. Kindle Edition.

Apathy is serious, but we can defeat it. Evagrius gives five unlikely cures for overcoming apathy.

The first is *tears*. Tears give us an emotional release. Any emotional experience, whether anger, laughter, love, or hatred, motivates us. Once our emotions are in gear, we are at least going somewhere. If we cry over our despair, we are at least acknowledging it and are likely to do something about it. But if we hide our feelings even from God, we are spinning our wheels and digging deeper into the mud of helplessness.

Second, Evagrius suggests *prayer*. Acknowledging God's existence means no situation is completely hopeless. God has promised never to leave or forsake us. (Hebrews 13:5, Jeremiah 29:11) With God on our side, we can never say any situation is hopeless. God is always ready to wake us up and give us a new purpose if we ask Him for help.

Third, Evagrius suggests *God's Word*. God's Word, the Bible, gives us promises that help us talk back to despair. Here are a few of them.

- "I will never leave you or forsake you" Hebrews 13:5.
- "I am with you always," Matthew 28:20.
- "I know the plans I have for you, plans for good and not for evil, to give you an end and a purpose." Jeremiah 29:11.
- "Delight yourself in the Lord, and He will give you the desires of your heart." Psalm 37:4

Fourth, Evagrius tells us to *get to work*! Sometimes, the only way to get through a rough patch is to keep working, whether or not we feel like working is pointless. Feelings are important, but they are often wrong. The only way to make progress is to keep going forward.

Psychiatrist M. Scott Peck, in his book *The Road Less Traveled,* talks about a woman he was treating who suffered from persistent depression and despair. Once she arrived at her appointment, she was full of excitement and energy. He asked her what made this day different.

The woman mentioned getting a call from her minister that morning. His car was in the shop, and he wondered if she would drive him around that day. She agreed and went with him to visit the sick, taking food to the poor, and so forth. She found it all exciting and worthwhile. Peck asked her.

"So why don't you do that more often? It seems to help you."

She was appalled. "What, you mean I would have to do it *every week?*" Despair was keeping her from committing to what she enjoyed.[10]

Evagrius' fifth solution is a shocker—*think about death!* Contemplating death makes us realize that life is too precious to waste.

In Ecclesiastes 12:1, we read. *"Remember your creator in the days of your youth, before the evil days come and the years approach when you will say, 'I have no pleasure in them.'"*. We plan for retirement, but do we plan spiritually for the future? When our strength and energy run out, can we still be happy? Can we still find enjoyment on the last day of our lives?

To prepare for death, we must live now. Despair snatches life away from us until we have never enjoyed what we were given. Our days are precious and few. We have no time to waste in hopelessness and despair. Contemplation of death causes us to appreciate the necessity of life.

---

[10] The Road Less Traveled: A New Psychology of Love, Traditional Values and Spiritual Growth (New York: Simon & Schuster, 1978).

Hope—the angel against Apathy

*"There remains three things—faith, **hope**, and love,"* I Corinthians 13:13. Hope is knowing that eventually we will see good come out of what we are doing.

Christianity is a hopeful religion. The Christian has three kinds of hope. The first is hope for heaven. A better life awaits us when we die.

Our second hope is that we can help bring a better world on earth. Paul said, *"Let us not be weary in well-doing, knowing we will reap in due time."* (Galatians 6:9). God has promised us that our work won't be worthless.

Our third hope is that we can have a happier life on Earth. Salvation does not just mean something for the next life but a happier life on earth. God has promised us a better, more fulfilling life here and now. Even just having hope makes us happier.

Many people find this third hope to be the hardest. There are a lot of poor, helpless people who follow the Lord. Meanwhile, plenty of rich and famous people seemed to care nothing about following God. No wonder many people have difficulty seeing how God can offer hope for this world. Life can sometimes be unfair.

But looks are deceiving. Just because a person is rich and famous doesn't mean they are happy or more blessed than the poor. The blessed part of the life of the Christian is not that we get riches but that we do not need them to be happy. A blessed Christian needs nothing to be happy.

The apostle Paul is a good example of this. Paul was born into a wealthy and influential family. He received the best education money could buy. He landed an important job working for the Sanhedrin- the Jewish governing body at the time. When he became a Christian, he lost all his advantages and privileges. He was beaten, stoned, and left for dead on numerous occasions. He lost all his money. Yet near the end of his life, he wrote in Philippians 4:12-13 *"I have learned the secret of being content in any and every situation, whether well fed or hungry, whether living in plenty or want. I can do all this through him who gives me strength."* Paul realized he did not need money, power, or security to be happy. He was content with what the Lord gave him.

We have to endure much in this world, but we do not have to be unhappy while we do it. We find a happy life in God's presence. Our happiness can improve right now. Hope doesn't come from what we have or whom we know but from God. As long as Christ is with us, hope is all around us. We can discover new joys and hopes today.

Pride

"Humble yourselves, therefore, under God's mighty hand, that he may lift you up in time. Cast all your anxiety on him because he cares for you.:6" I Peter 5: 6

Finally, we come to *pride.*
This is going to be a long one.
Most scholars regard pride as the root cause of all other soul cancers. C. S. Lewis wrote, *"Pride is spiritual cancer: it eats up the possibility of love, contentment, or common sense."*[11]

Pride is different from vainglory in this way—vainglory is how we relate to others. Pride is how we see ourselves. It is an obsession with what we feel about ourselves. Pride is being obsessed with ourselves, our problems, and our achievements.

Vainglory makes us think about what others see in us. Pride doesn't care what others think. It only cares about the self. A person may sit alone in a room full of crowded people, not even noticing anyone else, and still be full of pride. It may manifest in a thousand ways, but it is invisible. It is how we see ourselves, an obsession with our soul.

Good Pride

We often use the word *pride* in a good way, as when we talk about national pride, school pride, or pride as a synonym for self-esteem. But how can pride be both good and evil?

Pride is rooted in healthy self-esteem. Healthy self-esteem comes from what God thinks of us. To Him, we are loveable.

---

[11] C. S. Lewis, Mere Christianity

He has given us some special and wonderful traits that we love using. God's gifts to us are tools to a happy workman. If we have a hammer, don't we enjoy hammering? We take pride in what we build and do. There is nothing wrong with taking pride in what we can do with what God gives us.

Christ said of His relationship with us, "Come to me, all who labor and are heavily laden, and I will give you rest. Take my yoke upon you, and learn from me, for I am gentle and lowly in heart, and you will find rest for your souls. For my yoke is easy, and my burden is light." (Matt. 11:28–30) This is the only place in the Bible where Jesus tells us about His heart.[12]

But God's love for us does not mean He loves us more than others. He has given each person different tools, not better ones. Other people have different abilities, but each one has a use. He also gives us different tasks, but all our tasks are good. He gave some people strength, intelligence, mental stability, and charm to make everything in life easy. To other people, he gave apparent disabilities, both physically and emotionally, and life is hard for them. But which of the two deserves the most praise—the person who lived an easy, untroubled life or the one who overcame hard obstacles?

If you are not up to the abilities of your peers, or if you have abilities beyond your peers, you have no advantage over your peers in God's eyes, no matter what the world says. Our culture is deeply soaked in the sin of pride. We cannot live in this world as Christians and act like the world. We must rise above the world and see ourselves as valuable to Him, forgetting what the world may say. We cannot think of ourselves as better than others since we are not the same as others. We can only see our true worth in our relationship with God.

---

[12] Ortlund, Dane C.. Gentle and Lowly (pp. 17-18). Crossway. Kindle Edition.

As wonderful as this feeling of being loved is, it is not intended to be something we dwell upon. This does not mean the feeling should ever go away. Unlike some emotions we discussed, such as fear, anger, shame, etc., being loved was intended to be permanent and foundational to everything else we go through.

Feeling God's love leads us to love others. Being loved by God means that we can forget ourselves, not remember ourselves.

Bad Pride

Bad pride is known as *narcissism,* which is an obsession with self.

Narcissism comes from the Greek myth of Narcissus, a beautiful man lost in his reflection in a pool. The narcissist can never look at anything without seeing themselves. Whenever they meet another, the first question on their minds is, "What does this person think of me?"

Narcissists can be divided into three groups:

Obvious narcissists wave their egos in front of them wherever they go. They always draw attention to themselves, talk about themselves, and are obsessed with themselves. We normally think about them when we say someone is "egotistical" or "stuck up." It is not usually hard to spot these people.

Of the three, this kind is the least dangerous. You can usually spot them from a mile away. Though they are self-absorbed, they are not necessarily cruel or jealous. They can even be generous when it draws attention to themselves. An example is a rich man who donates to a college, if they will name a dorm after him. We may find them irritating, but they are relatively harmless.

Bashful narcissists are quiet and often withdrawn. These people are not stuck on their abilities, just on themselves. They never think of anyone else because they are too absorbed in their troubles. Hiding in fear is just as selfish as someone who is constantly bragging.

Then there are the *social narcissists*. Social narcissists seem to be focused on others but are really focused on themselves. Their social media posts often reflect all the many causes and charitable deeds they do. But they constantly post selfies of themselves doing it. Whatever they do is always more important than what anyone else does. They masquerade as do-gooders, but it is only the good they pursue. Politicians are always this way. They seem to be working "for the people," but it is the votes they are after.

Pride always comes back to the same thing—ourselves. Whether we think about how great or poor we are, it is the self we seek.

Pride has always been the most dangerous of the seven deadly sins because it is the hardest to spot. Even when we notice our pride and repent of it, we return to self-admiration by saying, "Look how humble I am."

To conquer pride, we must forget ourselves. This means cultivating an attitude of humility.

Humility---the angel against pride

Humility is not something we feel but something we don't feel. Humility is forgetting ourselves. Pride is seeking ourselves. Humility is thinking of others as greater than ourselves.

The Bible teaches us two important lessons about humility. The first is that humility is a choice. Here are some verses about humility.

Humble yourselves in the presence of the Lord, and He will exalt you. James 4:10

Therefore, humble yourselves under the mighty hand of God, that He may exalt you at the proper time. 1 Peter 5:6

Whoever exalts himself shall be humbled, and whoever humbles himself shall be exalted. Matthew 23:12.

Humbling ourselves means that we forget ourselves. When dealing with God, we forget ourselves and serve Him. When dealing with our leaders, police, pastors, teachers, employers, etc., we put their wishes above our own. Instead of focusing on our accomplishments, we should think about the accomplishments of others. Instead of our pains, think about others' pains, and so on. When we have achieved humility, we have forgotten ourselves so completely that we do not know we have accomplished it!

Second, humility is the way to influence the world. These passages all say the same thing—that the reward of humility is influence. We read about Jesus in Philippians 2: 5-11

> *In your relationships with one another, have the same mindset as Christ Jesus:*
> *Who, being in very nature God, did not consider equality with God something to be used to his own advantage; rather, he made himself nothing by taking the very nature of a servant, being made in human likeness. And being found in appearance as a man, He humbled himself by becoming obedient to death—even death on a cross!*
> *Therefore, God exalted him to the highest place and gave him the name that is above every name,*
> *That at the name of Jesus, every knee should bow, in heaven and on earth and under the earth,*
> *And every tongue acknowledge that Jesus Christ is Lord, to the glory of God the Father.*

Jesus wasn't just given the position of king of kings; He earned it by being humble. Jesus cared more about serving others than serving Himself. As a result, God lifted him above others. He earned his position by being humbled on the cross. He led by example.

Humility is won by doing, not seeking. It is not something we try to do; instead, we earn it by making other people more important than ourselves. This care and concern for others gives us tremendous power to change the world. Through humility, the meek will inherit the earth.

Third (and this is the most amazing part), humility is fun!

When we forget ourselves, we can experience the lives of everyone around us. We can enjoy their accomplishments as much as our own. We listen to their stories and rejoice with them. Instead of being bound by our joys and accomplishments, we expand our joy to include what others say or do.

I ask you, does humility make you smaller or greater? Does enjoying the lives of others and rejoicing in what they do mean less joy in life or more?

Narcissism is so restricting! It is like living with a fog over your face. You do not see the beautiful life around you. But living in humility is living with our eyes open. We can see the beautiful world of other people around us. Each person we meet becomes a great story, an epic adventure of discovery. Living within ourselves makes us smaller, not larger. The more we focus on ourselves, the less of the world we see. Only when we seek humility can we enter the larger world.

Epilogue—The Battle for the Soul

When we read what the ancient writers said about bad thoughts, we can't escape the fact that they actually believed in the Devil and demons. To them, soul cancers were not just a thought disease but an attack from two outside forces. Bad thoughts come from cultural forces because all human cultures are driven more by satanic forces than by the holy. We are all sinners; even when we hide our bad thoughts behind a Christian veneer, they are still wrong. The second outside force is the demons themselves, who put temptations in our minds at every turn. They stir up pride, grief, despair, and panic, where God plants humility, joy, hope, and courage. Not all bad thoughts come from demons, of course. Physical causes, trauma, and circumstances cause some people to be more susceptible than others to certain bad thoughts. But even if we had perfect brain chemistry and childhoods, we can still have bad thoughts. Just like physical cancers affect otherwise healthy people, soul cancers happen to people who do everything right.

Modern people do not generally believe in Satan or demons. But why not? Suppose we believe God reveals Himself directly to our inner self through the Holy Spirit. Why is it difficult to believe that there could be other spirits capable of speaking directly to our inner self? If we believe in angels, why should we not also believe in devils? C.S. Lewis said that the greatest power the Devil has over us is that we do not believe in him.

The early church believed in the Devil and demons, making exorcism a part of the usual baptism ceremony. According to the *Apostolic Tradition,* a Second Century primer on church practices, baptism was always preceded by a prayer for exorcism—that the new Christian would be saved from bad thoughts and addictions placed upon them by the Devil. [13]

God makes it impossible for a Christian to be possessed by the Devil, but that doesn't mean devils cannot influence our thoughts and actions. Satan bullies us with impure and obsessive thoughts and feelings. We must directly confront the evil spirits if we are to defeat soul cancers.

The Christian who wants to live a healthy life must face three enemies: our flesh--our fallen nature; the world--the culture of broken people around us, and unseen spiritual forces--the Devil and all his demons. We are no match for even one of them. That is why only Dr. Jesus can remove our soul cancers.

So, how do we call on Dr. Jesus?

Admit we have a problem with bad thoughts. Stop lying to yourself. Not all our feelings are justified. The world is not the cause of our problems—they are mostly our feelings. The reason we are afraid isn't that the world is scary. It is because we let fear tell us what to do. The reason we are in despair is because we have lost hope. Other people with worse problems are happier than we are because they still have hope. The reason we are so angry at people who hurt us is not because we have been hurt more than others but because we haven't learned to forgive. We don't have to solve our problems, however. We have to admit we have them.

Read the instructions. Read God's word, the Bible. Why? Because the Bible teaches us what good thinking looks like. Daily Bible reading isn't just some magic ritual that casts out spirits but a way of reshaping our thoughts and feelings to God's thoughts

---

[13] Baptism was (and still is in the Catholic Church), preceded by several minor "exorcisms," where priest or bishop prayed prayers over the catechumen about to be baptized, freeing them from any attachment to sin. How was baptism practiced in the early Church? (aleteia.org)

and feelings.

Today, we are all well aware of how the news shapes our perceptions of the world. If we watch only one news station, we get only one side of an issue. Our thoughts and feelings about what is happening in politics and culture are shaped by the source of learning we use. If we go to college, we will likely come out thinking like our professors do. If we read only books with a secular perspective, we will naturally assume God has no place in our thought life. But if we read the words that come from God daily, we will naturally come to see things the way God does. His thoughts become our thoughts. His love becomes our love.

We turn our soul cancers over to God in prayer. Here is the greatest thought you can ever have. *God exists.* God is not a product of human imagination but a real being in another dimension, which we call "heaven." He speaks to us in many ways, but He is always there. Although we are not normally given the ability to see Him as He is in that extra-dimensional space, He does reveal Himself to us. He revealed Himself in human form in the First Century in the form of Jesus Christ. Through Christ's teachings and actions, He revealed what a perfect life is like, not ruled by soul cancers. He revealed His love to us by dying on the cross as an atonement for all our sins. On the cross, He signed a peace treaty with us in his own blood to show how much He loved us. He wrote a pardon to us for all who have allowed our bad thoughts to control us. He forgave us so that even when our bad thoughts improve, He never leaves or forsakes us.

God also speaks to us through the Holy Spirit. This is God manifesting Himself in our thoughts and our world. When our problems overwhelm us, He answers our prayers. When our fears cause us to panic, He gives us the courage to hang on by faith. He gives us more when we think we will run out of our daily bread.

All the soul cancers come down to whether we believe God will provide. Greed, fear, despair, and pride come from an inner sense of inadequacy—*Can I trust God to give me what I need? Can I trust Him to protect me? Does He love me even when I have sinned? Am I worth anything in His eyes?* The answer to all these questions is an overwhelming "Yes!"

Do not be fooled—we can never eliminate our bad thoughts. But bad thoughts do not run us. They are cancers, but they are not fatal. Listen to these final words from I Corinthians 10:1: "*No temptation has overtaken you except what is common to humanity. And God is faithful; he will not let you be tempted beyond what you can bear. But when you are tempted, he will also provide a way out so that you can endure it.*"

Soul cancers come to us, but we do not have to despair. You can always go to Dr. Jesus.

Prayer for Deliverance

My Lord Jesus
By Your love, by Your Blood, and by Your power,
Release me from the bad thoughts which oppress my
inner life:
From the hunger of the belly that I may be temperate
From the need to possess that I may be generous
From the tyranny of lust that I may stay chaste
From the yearning for others' approval so I may live
honestly
From anger and resentment that I may forgive
From the power of shame that I may be grateful
From the prison of fear that I may have courage
From the darkness of grief that I may have joy
From the illusion of despair that I might have hope
From the poison of pride that I may be humble
Keep me, O Father, to my true intention--
To desire You, love You, and serve You
above all else forever,
in this world and the next.

Bad Thoughts Vs. Good Virtues

Gluttony	Temperance
Greed	Generosity
Sexual Desire	Chastity
Vainglory	Empathy
Anger	Forgiveness
Shame	Gratitude
Fear	Courage
Nostalgia	Joy
Despair	Hope
Pride	Humility

Made in the USA
Middletown, DE
05 November 2023

41856190R00066